CAT
FACTS

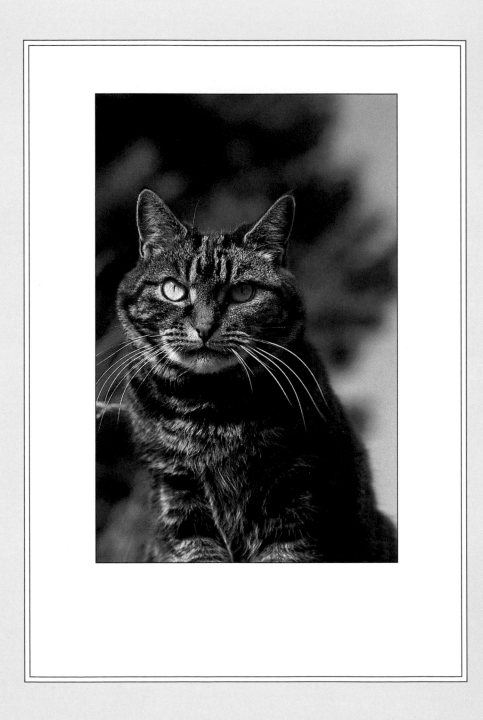

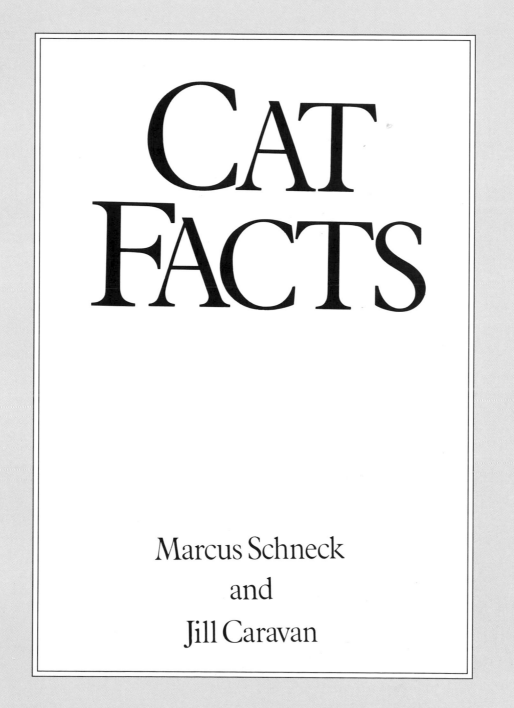

CAT FACTS

Marcus Schneck
and
Jill Caravan

Grange BOOKS

A QUANTUM BOOK

Published by Grange Books
An imprint of Grange Books plc
The Grange
Grange Yard
London SE1 3AG

Copyright © 1990 Quarto Publishing plc

Reprinted 1996

ISBN 1-85627-844-1

This book was produced by
Quantum Books Ltd
6 Blundell Street
London N7 9BH

Senior Editor Susanna Clarke

Art Editor Anita Ruddell

Designer Hazel Edington, Frances Austen

Illustrator (Cat Breeds) John Francis

Other Illustrators David Kemp, Sandra Pond, Will Giles

Picture Manager Joanna Wiese

Art Director Nick Buzzard

Publishing Director Janet Slingsby

Quarto would also like to thank the following for their
assistance: King and King, Karin Skånberg, Vana Haggerty
Angela Gair

Typeset by Ampersand Typesetting (Bournemouth) Ltd
Printed in Singapore by Star Standard Industries Pte. Ltd.

CONTENTS

WHEN AND WHERE DID CATS ORIGINATE?

THE CAT IS a mammal – a relatively small class of animals with self-regulating body temperature, hair, and, in the females, milk-producing mammae. There are about 15,000 species of mammals out of a few million total species of animals.

Following the evolutionary chain that gave rise to all life, the first mammals evolved from reptiles about 200 million years ago. But it was not until about 70 million years ago that the mammals began to assume the dominant role they currently hold. They also began to develop into the many families that exist today.

Several early carnivore (meat-eating) groups arose to fill the niche of hunter, among them the *Miacis*. At first the *Miacis* were small, weasel-like animals, but they had the necessary equipment to survive and develop further, while other, competing groups fell into extinction. As the evolutionary processes acted on them, offering them ever-wider niches to fill, about 45-50 million years ago they developed into the ancestors of today's carnivore families, including cats.

Spurred on by their hunting prowess, the cats spread quickly and further evolved into many different forms that could best take advantage of localized prey and environment. Few of these evolutionary "experiments" survive today. It's been at least 13,000 years since the sabre-tooth tiger – once spread across the globe – has walked the earth. The giant tiger of Asia and the cave lion of Europe are likewise gone, probably becoming extinct even before the sabre-tooth.

The first ancestors of the modern cat apparently lived at the same time as these now extinct animals but were better able to take advantage of their situation and

Right: *Prehistoric skull of the fearsome* Smilodon, *or sabre-tooth cat, an early form of feline that existed until about 13,000 years ago. To accommodate the huge upper canine teeth, which were used to stab prey and then tear it apart, the jaws could open to 90 degrees.*

Dinictis Existed until 40 million years ago. About the size of a lynx. Long upper canines used to stab prey.

Pseudaelurus These animals more closely resembled today's cats, with long limbs and five-toed feet. They began to die out 25 million years ago.

continue on. The oldest known fossilized record with a strong similarity to today's cats has been dated as from about 12 million years ago.

As recently as three million years ago the earth was shared by many more, distinct varieties of cat than the four genera that we recognize today: *Panthera*, the big cats such as lions; *Felis*, the smaller cats, that cannot roar; *Neofelis*, the Clouded Leopard; and, *Acinonyx*, only the cheetah, that has claws that cannot fully retract.

It is generally agreed that about 40 different species of cat exist today. The domestic cat is just one of them, but with man's help it has developed greater variety than all the others. While colouration and pattern of coat have evolved in wild cats only so far as needed to camouflage them from their prey and their competition, controlled breeding has introduced dramatic variations in the physical features of domestic cats that are unrelated to evolution or their environment.

Man has also spread the cat to the few parts of the Earth that Nature had not already taken it. By two million years ago, cats had settled on nearly every continent. Continental drift brought North and South America back into contact and gave the southern land mass its first cats. But many islands, such as the Galápagos Group off the coast of South America, had no feline predators until the past few centuries, when man arrived and brought domestic cats with him. These new carnivores meant disaster for the native wildlife there. Likewise Australia had no cats until man brought them there. Antarctica remains catless, apart from any pets that research teams bring with them.

Today's cats are divided into three genera: Acinonyx, ***above*** *the cheetah, which has claws that cannot be fully retracted;* Felis, ***right*** *the small cats, including our many domestic breeds; and* Panthera, ***left*** *the great cats, like the lions.*

Below: *The ancestors of the cat.*

Felis lunensis The first true cats, similar in size to the small Wild Cats of today. Existed until 12 million years ago.

Felidae Carnivorous mammals and highly efficient hunters.

WHO DOMESTICATED THE CAT?

AS MAN BECAME aware of the value that different animals could have for him, he began to domesticate them. Dogs made excellent hunting partners. Cows provided meat, milk, and labour. Horses were a fine form of transportation.

It was the cats, however, that decided to live with man, not the other way around. What attracted cats to man was the hordes of rats and mice that congregated around the stores of food that man had learned to build up in ancient Egypt.

The cats that first chose to live near or with man, and thus became the ancestors of all domestic breeds, were of the African Wild Cat species (*Felis lybica*) that still exists today.

The earliest known evidence of a cooperative relationship between man and cat has been dated at 4,500 years ago. It came in the form of cat images painted on tomb walls, carved and moulded statues of cats, and even mummified remains of cats.

Egyptian religion included cat images among other sacred symbols even before cats had claimed the granaries as their hunting grounds. They believed that their gods took on the appearance of cats in order to pass down orders and omens. Priests had previously worshipped the lion, but that was a large and dangerous animal. Now, in these smaller, vermin-hunting felines they found a more pleasing symbol. These forerunners of the domestic cat weren't the tame creatures we know today, but in comparison with lions they were quite manageable.

As each new generation of cat (and there were many under the newly found protection of man) demonstrated greater domestication, the animals came to share the homes of the Egyptians.

Despite their domesticity, they did not lose their sacred status. To kill a cat was a crime punishable by death. The felines were embalmed and mummified when they died, and embalmed mice were placed with them in their tombs. Families mourned the deaths of cats that had shared their homes as they mourned the deaths of human family members. In one ancient city unearthed in the late 1800s, more than 300,000 mummified cat remains were found.

The Greeks were the first Europeans to recognize the mousing value of these Egyptian felines, and when the Egyptians wouldn't trade any of their sacred cats, the Greeks stole several pairs. And the Greeks gradually sold the offspring of these cats to their traditional trading partners, the Romans, Gauls, and Celts.

The vermin-control abilities of the cat continued to be appreciated, and man spread the animal throughout

Below: *This ancient Egyptian bronze figurine wearing gold earrings was dedicated to the cult of Bast, goddess of fertility and love. The ancient Egyptians were the first to tame the cat. Used at first as a hunter and retriever, it was later valued as a pet, and finally became an object of worship.*

the civilized world, although not without setbacks. It was unfortunate that the Church decided to condemn the rat-killing cat as a pagan symbol during the Middle Ages, as rats were spreading the Plague that would eventually kill millions throughout Europe. Persecution of the felines was widespread. The Festival of St. John was annually celebrated with the burning alive of cats in town squares. By 1400 the species was nearly extinct.

It was not until it became apparent that certain physical and mental conditions were not caused by witches (who it was believed regularly transformed themselves into cats), that cats began to grow popular once again in Europe.

Right: Life is good for the vast majority of domestic cats today, and they are kept as pets in huge numbers all over the world. Ironically, their very popularity as pets has much to do with their independence of spirit and the fact that the wild, "untamed" side of their natures is never far below the surface.

Left: During the Middle Ages cats were persecuted as agents of Satan, but happily this situation was reversed in the 17th century when they achieved new-found respect due to their ability to control plague-bearing rats. By the 18th century, cats were highly prized as pets among the European intelligentsia and began to be featured in paintings and literature. This oil painting, Stable Animals, is by an anonymous mid-19th century English artist.

HOW MANY CAT BREEDS ARE THERE?

FOR THE FIRST several thousand years of their association with man, cats were functional animals kept for their mousing abilities or were pets kept mainly for their companionship. But it was only a matter of time until the feline's great natural diversity gave rise to the concept of breeding.

In the mid-19th century in Europe, particularly in Great Britain, owners began to take pride in the specific characteristics of their animals and to attempt to breed them to refine and enhance those characteristics. Proud owners had exhibited their cats as early as the 16th century, but the first show that could really be called a show by modern standards was held in 1871 at the Crystal Palace in London. There were 25 show classes, divided into either Eastern or British.

Initially, the breeding efforts focused upon those cats that had become native to the British Isles. But travellers were soon bringing back exotic-looking cats, first the Persians and later the Siamese.

Associations sprang up to oversee and regulate the breeding and showing activity. Founded in Britain in 1887 The National Cat Club was the first. Others followed and came together in 1910 as The Governing Council of the Cat Fancy. In 1983 a breakaway group formed the Cat Association of Britain.

Several similar organizations have developed in the United States. The American Cat Association is the oldest, but the Cat Fanciers' Association is the largest. Others include the American Cat Fanciers' Association, Cat Fanciers' Federation, Crown Cat Fanciers' Federation, United Cat Federation, and International Cat Association.

The Canadian Cat Association is the governing body for Canada, while the Fédération Internationale Féline de l'Europe is the largest in continental Europe.

Not all organizations recognize the same breeds. For example, only a few U.S. organizations recognize the hairless Sphynx, and while the Scottish Fold is recognized in the United States, it is not officially recognized by the Governing Council in Britain.

Despite the differences, or maybe because of them in some instances, about 100 pedigree breeds are now recognized. That number reflects duplication in that some major organizations classify some breeds dif-

Below: Domestic short haired cats are charming, intelligent, loyal and adaptable; they make ideal family pets.

Right: Long-haired cats, such as this Blue-Cream, are considered by many to be the most beautiful family of felines.

ferently. All breeds generally fall into one of four categories: Longhairs, Siamese, Shorthairs, and Foreign Shorthairs. However, that is far from an all-inclusive total.

Some breeds, such as the Snowshoe, are so new that breed standards have not been fully developed to allow for their official recognition. Others, such as the Sphynx and Scottish Fold, remain highly controversial, with some strong feelings against even continuing these lines.

Today, Persians are the most popular breed – if measured in sheer numbers of cats entered into shows – in the cat fancy, the term that covers the breeding and judging of pedigreed cats. The enthusiasts of most other breeds would naturally argue the point.

But the cat fancy encompasses only a small minority of the many millions of owners of cats; they may be the most vocal owners in favour of their own particular breed, but they are a minority nonetheless.

Much of the rest of our large fraternity of cat owners would be hard pressed to classify their cat or cats any further than feline. There's no need. Pedigree or moggie (the term for a nonpedigree cat), the cat that shares the house with you is without a doubt the best cat on the face of the Earth. In addition, many cat clubs provide for the showing of nonpedigree, well-cared for, and well-groomed house cats or crossbreeds that cannot be placed in a specific breed class.

Another consideration, of course, is the cost. Moggies are available for free at all times. Animal shelters have more than they can ever place; advertisements in newspapers constantly offer free cats to good homes. Pedigrees, on the other hand, carry a price tag that generally reflects the fame and fortunes of the cat's bloodline, and the effort that has gone into building that line. While most of these prices are not all that high, some sought-after, champion-line kittens fetch prices that will turn a head or two. For some particularly unusual varieties there are even waiting lists of several years.

The 100 breeds that exist today should not be considered the final number of breeds. The past few decades have seen the creation of several new ones, and there are probably more to come.

Below: The Siamese is one breed that most people can identify on sight. They are extremely popular pedigree cats, *for apart from their beauty and grace, they have intelligence, resourcefulness and a delightful disposition.*

Below: Cats fall into three main groupings, according to body type:

Cobby type with compact body, deep chest, short legs and broad head. The eyes are large and round

Muscular type with sturdy body and round, full-cheeked head.

Foreign type with slender body and long legs and tail. The head is wedge-shaped, with tall ears and slanting eyes.

HAVE ANY BREEDS DISAPPEARED?

HAVE YOU EVER seen a Mexican Hairless? Not the nicknamed dog, but the specific breed of cat? Probably not. It is a lost breed, bred only briefly in the late 1800s in Mexico.

The Mexican Hairless is one lost breed that we know about. There have been others, lost because of lack of interest and for other reasons. But how many potential breeds have been lost without the cat fancy even knowing about them?

Although mutations are not commonplace, every-day happenings, they do occur regularly enough for us to be certain that many more than have been made public have actually appeared in litters around the world. Perhaps owners failed to recognize the potential in the mutation, or even destroyed the "different" animal. Perhaps pressure to destroy it was put on them by local cat owners. For whatever reasons, they kept the mutation to themselves and it was lost – at least for the time – with the death of an individual cat.

For example, a white variety of the Russian Blue was bred experimentally for a time in Great Britain. But, due to lack of widespread interest, much of the breeding programme has been dropped, and the variety is now quite rare.

The human whim has also brought some breeds that are widespread and popular today to near extinction. When the Persian was first gaining popularity among the cat fancy in Great Britain, it did so primarily at the expense of the closely related Turkish Angora. As a result, the Turkish Angora was slowly moving towards extinction.

However, more recent popularity in the United States has brought the Turkish Angora a new lease of life. The breed is in the midst of a major revival, freshened with new blood from cats imported from the Ankara Zoo in Turkey.

Conversely, popularity almost drove the Siamese into extinction. As the breed became fashionable in the

1920s, breeders were hard pressed to keep up with demand. As a result they took shortcuts, including repeated inbreeding, that nearly destroyed the blood lines. In the nick of time, some breeders recognized the threat to the breed and reinstituted the careful breeding procedures needed to ensure the continuation of a strong, healthy breed.

The Abyssinian came similarly close to the brink of disappearance much more recently, albeit not because of its popularity. During World War I and World War II, food scarcities struck everywhere in the European community. Meat, the essential dietary item of the Abyssinian (even more so than many other breeds), was in short supply, even for human consumption.

The breed was nearly extinct at the close of World War II. It had made a recovery by the 1960-70s, but then it was devastated by mass outbreaks of the feline leukaemia virus. Although it is rather rare, the Abyssinian is an extremely popular cat and is now enjoying another strong period of recovery.

A look into the future of cat breeds is as simple as a visit to the section of any well-stocked pet shop that houses hamsters, guinea pigs and mice. There you'll find new coat types that mutation has yet to produce in cats or that man has yet to decide to encourage.

Perhaps the next breed of cat will have the rosette coat, with hair growing outward in all directions from various starting points across the body. Or, maybe the satin coat, with its light-reflecting hairs, will capture a group of supporters.

When you consider how far we have come in just over 100 years, from the first cat show at the Crystal Palace in 1871 with its 25 different judging classes, nothing seems impossible.

Opposite page: This 17th-century Flemish painting depicts a strange, moustachioed cat with an unnervingly "human" face.

Left: The history of the Chartreuse goes back to 1558, when it was reportedly bred in France by monks at the Monastery of La Grande Chartreuse. The breed has now been amalgamated with the British Blue, known in the United States as Exotic Shorthair Blue.

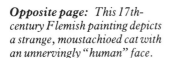

Below: The Angora is one of the most ancient breeds, named after Angora (now Ankara), the capital city of its native country. It first reached Europe in the 16th century, where it was highly acclaimed.

Below: Although strikingly similar in appearance to the sacred cats of the Egyptian Pharaohs, it is considered unlikely that the Abyssinian is a direct descendant.

WHAT IS A PEDIGREE?

THE PEDIGREE CERTIFICATE is the key to every bit of record-keeping that is so vital to planned cat breeding, breeding that will produce desired results. The certificate authenticates a specific cat as a full-fledged member of its breed. Most go back over four generations of the cat's parentage, although some organizations require as many as seven.

The pedigree is a natural step in a progression that began with the first cat shows in the mid-19th century. Owners began to have pride in their pets, to try to arrive at the "perfect" design for their pets, and finally to exhibit their results for others to see – and compete with.

Establishing standards of excellence for the "ideal" animal was the natural next step, followed by pedigree records as the means to authenticate and trace ancestry. But the pedigree certificate is much more than a guide to the past. In the hands of a knowledgeable and skilled breeder, it can be like a fine dessert recipe in the hands of a master chef. There, in the cat's ancestry the breeder can learn of the recessive genes that the animal carries and can pass on to its genetic heirs. The breeder can also learn of the amount of inbreeding that has taken place in the cat's ancestors and the animal's relationship to other, possibly noted and prized, bloodlines.

A pedigree with gaps can be like a recipe with key ingredients not listed. The result of breeding the animal, or making the dessert, is anyone's guess. And, of course, just as in making a fine dessert, variables will enter into the process occasionally, giving us something that no one could have anticipated. Mutation is one of those variables in breeding. It is explained more fully under the section on selective breeding.

Exactly when a breed or variety gets its official "papers" depends on the registering organization, of which we've already explained there may be quite a few. Some allow kittens to be registered to ensure that there will be proper record-keeping for several years prior to being admitted to show. Others demand that several generations of the potential new breed first be produced. Still others insist that a certain number of cats or breeders be involved with a new breed before it can be recognized.

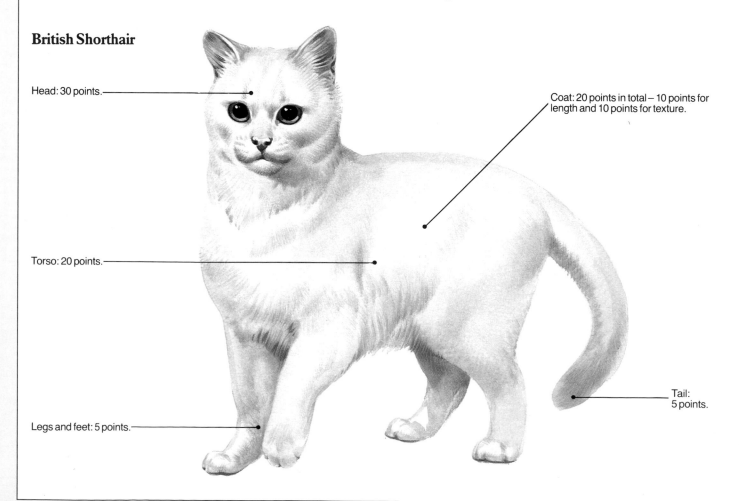

British Shorthair

Head: 30 points.

Coat: 20 points in total – 10 points for length and 10 points for texture.

Torso: 20 points.

Legs and feet: 5 points.

Tail: 5 points.

Above: *The pedigree certificate on this Blue-Cream Longhair will reveal a great deal about its blood line, as well as its breeding potential.*

Left: *Two Silver tabbies. On the left is a classic (blotched) tabby; on the right is a spotted tabby. The pedigree tabby pattern is strictly laid down, and is not possessed by the common-or-garden tabby we all know and love. The price of a purebred cat varies according to the breed, the quality of the pedigree, and the beauty of the parents.*

Below and below left: *For each particular breed of pedigree cat there is a system of points for judging at shows. The total number of points is 100 and a maximum is set for specific features. The two cats shown here are **left** the British Shorthair and **right** the Maine Coon.*

Maine Coon

Head: 30 points in total – 15 points for the shape, 10 points for the ears and 5 points for the eyes.

Body: 35 points in total – 20 points for the shape, 5 points for the neck, 5 points for the legs and feet and 5 points for the tail.

Colour: 15 points

Coat: 20 points in total – 10 points for the length and 10 points for the texture.

HOW DOES SELECTIVE BREEDING WORK?

TO THE AVERAGE person, selective breeding is a collection of poorly understood terms and concepts that often seem best left to those who are willing to devote their lives to it. However, selective breeding relies on a few basic concepts as its starting points, concepts that we can all easily grasp.

These concepts were first discovered in the mid-19th century by an Austrian monk by the name of Johann Gregor Mendel. Using common garden peas, Mendel was the first person to look at how inherited traits are passed from parent to offspring. He learned that certain patterns of inheritance recur with predictable consistency. He put forth two "laws" that then fell into obscurity until their rediscovery in the early 1900s.

Mendel's first law states that if two parents of pure strains are crossed and they differ in only one trait, for which one has two dominant factors (his word for genes), and the other one has two recessive factors, all the offspring of the first generation will display the dominant factor trait. For example, the crossing of a true-breeding black-coated parent and a true-breeding blue-coated parent will result in black-coated kittens. Black is dominant over blue.

His second law states that crossing of the offspring will then produce variety in that same trait. Some will look like each of the grandparents in terms of that trait and some will look like neither. Continuing with our example, some of the next generation will have black coats, some blue coats and some will have other-type coats.

Today we understand the inner workings of what Mendel was observing. All features of any cat, any living creature for that matter, are controlled by genes, which are situated on chromosomes. When fertilization takes place, the sperm cell from the male unites with the egg cell from the female, and the chromosomes of the created offspring are arranged in pairs. Half of each pair comes from the father, while the other half comes from the mother. Thus, the newly created animal is given its genetic programming; its features have been determined.

Following these laws, which since Mendel's time have been much further developed, breeders attempt to produce kittens with top show potential by continuing the best features of the parents and improving on other features. They can concentrate entirely on the aesthetic qualities, because usefulness of the animal in terms of a function need not be considered.

New breeds and varieties are established in one of three ways:

- Mutation – this was responsible for beginning breeds such as the Sphynx, American Wirehair, Cornish Rex, and Devon Rex. Initial occurrences of a mutation are impossible to predict, but when they do occur they are passed on to subsequent generations like any other gene.

- Recombination of mutant genes – this generally gives us new colour varieties rather than entirely new breeds. It is how breeders eventually developed a dozen varieties of the Burmese.

- Ongoing selection of the polygenes (also called the quantitative genes) that produce the desired characteristic – no mutation is involved, only the selection for further breeding of the members from each new generation that best demonstrate the desired characteristic. The Siamese has undergone this man-made process for many generations.

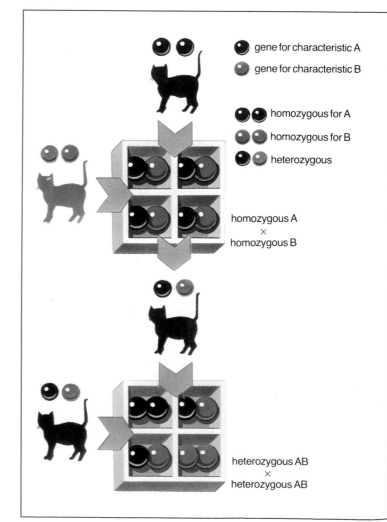

gene for characteristic A

gene for characteristic B

homozygous for A

homozygous for B

heterozygous

homozygous A
×
homozygous B

heterozygous AB
×
heterozygous AB

Mutation may explain the fact that kittens of domestic cats are born domestic. With most wild species, the domestication process must be repeated with each new generation. But domestic kittens are tame from birth. Somewhere in the domestic cat's relatively brief association with people the mutation arose that better adapted the animal for life with humans. Mutations that accommodate better adaptation are the only ones that generally persist into future generations.

Another important term in breeding is "inbreeding". Inbreeding is itself neither good nor bad. It is simply a process.

Breeders commonly use inbreeding to purify bloodlines, breeding the best to the best to get closer to that "ideal" cat. Inbred offspring resemble each other more with each new generation. However, caution must be exercised at every step along the way for inbreeding can bring out a harmful recessive mutant trait.

Above: A great many more cats are produced by chance than by planning, such as these feral cats taking advantage of a handout.

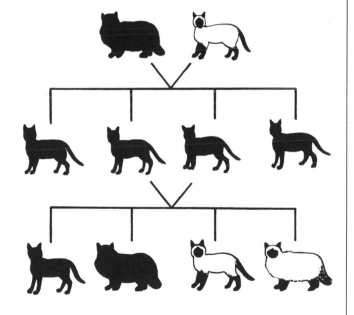

Left: Every physical characteristic of a cat is determined by two separate genes, one from each parent. For instance a particular pair will decide coat colour. A "pure bred" black has two genes for black coat colour and will produce black kittens. These "pure bred" black cats are said to be homozygous (breeding true). A pure-bred black mated with a pure-bred blue will also produce black kittens; this is because the black gene is "dominant" and the blue gene is "recessive". The kittens, with their inherited black and blue genes, are said to be heterozygous. A heterozygous cat can pass on the recessive gene to its offspring; when this recessive gene meets a second recessive gene passed on by the other parent, the recessive characteristic will once again assert itself. So when two black cats carrying the blue gene mate, some of their offspring are likely to be blue – though this is a matter of chance, and the result of any particular mating cannot be predicted.

Above: This family tree shows how cat breeders exploit their understanding of genetics to develop new breeds – in this case the aim is a long-haired cat with point colouring. A "pure bred" black longhair is crossed with a pointed shorthair. The genes for black colour and short hair are dominant and so all the kittens have these characteristics. However all the kittens also have genes for point colouring and long hair. When two of these kittens are crossed, the next generation could include cats with various permutations of the four characteristics, including some long-haired cats with point colouring.

Do Cats think?

ANYONE WITH MORE than passing contact with cats has probably known one that could tell when its owner was arriving home, open the door to get out, scratch on the window to get in, or perform some other feat that suggests that cats have something of note between their ears.

On the other hand, many of us have known a cat that seemed not able to respond to almost any stimuli, made a mess, or injured itself when it overstepped its intelligence bounds, never picked up any tricks, or never learned to make its needs known.

Obviously, there are smart cats, and there are not-so-smart cats. Like humans, for every cat that can accomplish a feat of great intelligence, there is another one that bungles it. But, as a species, there is no denying that cats are intelligent.

Of course, no one has yet developed an IQ test for cats or has been able to prove the claimed intellectual superiority of certain breeds, such as Siamese. But certain characteristics of cats lead us to believe that they can think.

One clue is their cautiousness. Many other animals are not smart enough to know when there could be danger. Another is their curiosity. They will explore things in situations not essential to their survival – a sure sign of intelligence far beyond the needs of mere existence. They also have a capacity for problem solving. Using their acute awareness of the world around them, they can work out answers to problems and then adapt solutions to different situations.

Cats are also independent-minded, with wills of their own. Unlike Pavlov's dogs, which repeat actions or press buttons so that they get a reward, many cats would sooner fall asleep than be involved in such experiments. Some of these cats may be judged as not very bright, or lazy, but arguably they are only exerting their independence and refusing to cooperate (see Can Cats Learn?).

Cats' brains, in order to stay active, need to process a constant flow of information and stimulation from their environments. Electroencephalogram (EEG) readings, recording the brain activity of cats in stimulus-free environments, showed that the cats' brains gradually shut down to a basic body-maintenance level, without storing any thoughts or ideas.

This experiment also explains why kittens whose senses are not "exercised" from an early age do not grow up to function normally. The most intelligent cats are those raised by people who handle them, play with them, and provide a variety of stimuli for their amusement and growth.

Above: As with young humans, life for the adolescent cat is an adventure and a time for discovering new experiences. Exploratory behaviour not only develops intelligence, but also physical fitness – and those important lightning reflexes.

Right: Thinking that no one is looking, this family cat seizes the chance of a few table scraps.

Left: *The inquisitiveness and playfulness of a kitten are highly appealing, but play also has a serious purpose, for it is through play that intelligence and survival skills develop. Faced with an unfamiliar object, this kitten approaches cautiously – displaying the feline's instinctive awareness of – and readiness to deal with – potential danger.*

CAT WATCHING TIP

Curiosity may have killed the cat, but it's also what leads it to learn about its environment and get what it wants. Show your cat what is in a full milk bottle. Then, after tightly sealing the bottle, leave the cat alone in the room with it. There will be lots of looking, then some sniffing, followed by some clawing and pawing, which will probably result in the bottle falling onto its side and the cat jumping back in surprise. Once it has recovered, the cat will again approach the bottle, this time more cautiously. Although the cat is interested in the entire bottle, it will likely focus its actions on the lid because it learned when you showed it the milk that that's how you get to it.

CAN CATS REMEMBER?

YOU MAY WANT your cat to remember that you don't want it to scratch the furniture. Or lie on your favourite black sweater. Or bring prey back to the house. You have made these requests clear to your cat time and again. And you are sure that if your cat had any capacity at all for memory it would remember these few simple rules. Wouldn't it?

Not necessarily. Cats have a great capacity for learning and memory, but they tend to save it for useful information – useful to them – and for their own gain or comfort, not yours. Cats remember what they like to eat and the location of their water dish; how to find a litter box and how to use it; the look, sound, and feel of their favourite toy or toys and where those objects are at any given moment; the taste of their favourite prey and the best location for stalking it; what to do when they tire, and the location of the sunniest, warmest, cosiest sleeping spot in the house.

They remember which of the noises they make are effective in getting their owners to respond to their various wants, and usually at mealtimes they remember their own names. Outside, they remember the location of their territory and that of other cats. And what things in the neighbourhood to avoid – like

Below: A place in the sun. Like those serious sunbathers you find on Mediterranean beaches, these cats don't seem to mind the overcrowded conditions in the sunniest, most popular locations.

puddles and dogs, in some cases. But their memory is selective, and only with proper training will they "remember" things you want them to know.

Aside from the mundane, some cats are known to have extraordinary "memories" for finding places. Taken away from their homes, they are able to remember where they live. (This doesn't work if a family moves, leaving the cat behind. The cat tracks down the place, not the people.)

The key to this homing ability is built-in celestial navigation, similar to that used by birds. During the time a cat lives in a particular house its brain automatically registers the angle of the sun at certain times of the day. Should a cat leave or be taken away from that house, it can find it again by using its internal biological clocks, through trial and error, to put the angle of the sun in the right place. It doesn't even need a clear day to navigate; it uses polarized light. This homing ability has also been attributed to cats' sensitivity to the Earth's magnetic fields. When magnets are attached to cats, their normal navigational skills are disrupted. Such navigation occurs in the subconscious, but eventually the cat finds itself in a neighbourhood that smells, looks, and sounds like its old area.

Cats can also remember people and animals they come into contact with. They will recognize who treats them well and who mistreats them. But, alas, a mother cat that meets up with one of her kittens later in life is not likely, or at least does not show the ability, to remember it as a creature she once carried inside her and fed.

Above: Most cats have an instinctive dislike of water, and do not like getting their paws muddy. Though their fur is a good insulator against the cold, it is not a very efficient "raincoat".

Left: Cats have a memory for things important to their lives, such as a prime mousing location.

CAT WATCHING TIP

Your cat's daily routine probably coincides with and, in some cases, depends on your schedule. It awakens when you do, goes to bed when you do, eats when you provide food, and goes out when you decide it's time. As it learns your routine, it picks up on preroutine signals, especially when the payoff is food or warmth.

Does your cat jump up on your bed to snuggle in for the night when it sees or hears you get into bed? Or is it already there when you turn in, having heard you turn off the TV or run the water to brush your teeth?

Does it come running when it hears the can opener? Or does it anticipate breakfast when you turn on the coffee-maker or emerge from the shower?

CAN CATS LEARN?

Above: *A mother leads her kittens on an early hunting trip, passing on the skills of reconnaissance and ambush required to take prey. Feline mothers are good teachers.*

Below: *Practising his hunting skills, this kitten crouches motionless, preparing to pounce. Cats are patient hunters and expert at concealment, staying in hiding for long periods until potential prey happens by.*

ALTHOUGH KITTENS SEEM to be born with some knowledge (see Do Cats Have Instincts?), there are many behaviours that they do, indeed, learn and many others that they can be taught.

Hunting is an example of learned behaviour. Queens allowed outdoors begin to bring back prey to the litter when the kittens are approximately three weeks old. At first, the mother will bring back dead prey and eat it while the kittens watch. Later she will bring live prey and kill it in front of them for them to eat. Eventually she will bring live prey for the kittens to kill. Kittens learn more quickly from their mothers than from the examples set by unrelated cats. Feline hunting is not instinctive, and kittens born of nonhunting mothers or without littermates may never learn to hunt.

Other habits, such as using a litter box, may also be learned from mother's example. Although kittens play in the litter, they don't know until they see their mother using the litter box that they are following the instinct to bury faeces to protect their trails from predators.

Cats can also be trained to perform, as long as trainers remember that cats like food, warmth, and company, and dislike water, loud noises, and cold – and *if* the cats feel like cooperating.

Cats can be taught to use a litter box or toilet, come when called, sit, beg, eat with paws, walk to heel on a

lead, jump through a hoop, play a piano, play dead, roll over, open a door (including a refrigerator door), hide food in boxes, shake, fetch, and many other tasks and feats. They can also be taught not to do things, like scratch furniture or hunt birds. They can be scared away with a "Shoo" or "No, no."

Necessary for training success is love for the animal, patience, consistency, authority, repetition, and rewards, but never punishment. A cat will not learn like a dog – no sharp vocal tones for *their* educational endeavours. These upset cats, making them fearful or aggressive and unsuitable for life with people.

Cats learn to keep doing things you want them to do, such as meowing to be let out, through rewards and reinforcement when they do them. But they do not learn not to do things you don't want them to do, such as scratching furniture, by having rewards refused to them. For these you must resort to gentle deterrents that are not directly associated with the owner; try a well-aimed ball of paper or squirt from a water pistol.

Cats can also learn their names if the names are simple and distinct. Cats respond especially well to names ending with an "ee" sound like "Kitty" or "Fluffy." To teach a kitten its name, call it before each meal so the sound will be associated with the pleasurable sensation of food. Reinforce with lots of attention.

Right: Kittens do not need a live target for hunting practice. Objects such as catnip mice, an empty cotton reel, or a screwed up piece of paper will be stalked, pounced upon and tossed into the air.

Below: At times the cat also becomes the hunted. Here, a red fox prepares to attack a cat.

CAT WATCHING TIP

Your cat's activities while outdoors on its own can tell you something about the hunting abilities of its immediate parents and more distant ancestors. While there are many distinctions that can be made between mother cats in their relationships with their kittens, one of the most interesting is that between hunting and nonhunting females.

Does the female bring half-dead mice and other rodents back to the kittens for them to practise their hunting skills? Or does she go through all the motions of the hunt without ever making a capture or kill and, so, passes no complete hunting abilities onto the kitten?

DO CATS DREAM?

Below: *Any sunny spot will do. Cats like to feel warm and secure before they will sleep. They will often change their sleeping position with the movement of the sun, to compensate for the slight drop in body temperature when sleeping.*

Right: *New-born kittens spend 90 percent of their time asleep, but by the age of three to four weeks this reduces to the adult level of around 60 percent.*

NOTHING CONVEYS A warm, cosy feeling more than the proverbial sight of the cat curled up and sleeping on a rug in front of the fire. Cats do sleep a lot – 16 to 18 hours a day, from 66 to 75 percent of each 24-hour period. Just how much cats sleep depends on their environment and how much companionship is available. Cats left on their own tend to sleep more than those who have company.

They will choose to sleep in any of many locations, but they are usually particularly attracted to soft, warm locations such as beds. Cats will move their sleeping spot with the sun to help counteract the slight fall in their body temperature when they are asleep.

Sleeping cats have been studied with electro-encephalograms (EEG) which read their brain activity. Phases of deep sleep and light sleep have been distinguished. During the day, sleep periods are light. The muscles are not totally relaxed, and the cat wakes periodically after only several minutes of sleep. This type of sleep, which makes up approximately 70 percent of cats' sleep time, gave rise to the term "cat naps," meaning brief periods of sleep.

After light sleep of up to about 30 minutes, cats may enter a deep sleep phase, which is revealed by a change in the EEG pattern. The eyes move rapidly in brief bursts during this deep sleep, although the eyelids remain closed. Because of such eye activity this deep

Above: *When a cat wakes, it goes through a leisurely yoga-like ritual, designed to loosen all the joints and muscles and get the* *circulation going. It gives a luxurious yawn, then stretches the front and back legs in turn and arches its back.*

Above: *Even when fast asleep, cats are still endearing. They will sleep on anything, but they like to feel safe and out of reach.*

sleep is also known as "rapid eye movement" (REM) sleep. About 30 percent of cats' sleep is REM sleep. Periods of REM sleep alternate with light sleep once the cycle has started.

During REM sleep there is external evidence, in addition to the eye movement, that cats do dream, or at least have semiconscious experiences similar to human dreams: there are changes in body posture, movement of paws and claws, twitching of whiskers, flicking of the ears, and in some cases, vocalization.

In deep sleep cats' brains are as active as when they are awake, and their senses are just as alert for incoming stimuli. So don't try to poke at cats or pull their tails while they are napping – they will respond accordingly. This applies to positive stimuli as well; try waving a dish of your cat's favourite food under its nose while it's sleeping.

Whether cats dream or not, REM sleep is an important biological function, and REM-sleep-deprived cats "catch up" on REM sleep as soon as they have a chance.

CAT WATCHING TIP

Compare sleeping positions with this chart that correlates position with electroencephalogram (EEG) readings.

Your cat is most alert when awake (1), but its brain waves slow down and get larger as it falls into light sleep, maybe sitting or partially lying down (2). Getting really comfortable and falling into a deep sleep (3)

results in a physically very relaxed cat, but one whose brain waves are similar to those when the cat is awake. Positions alternate as the cat drifts in and out of light and deep sleep (4), before it awakens and returns to its upright position and its normal waking brain waves (5).

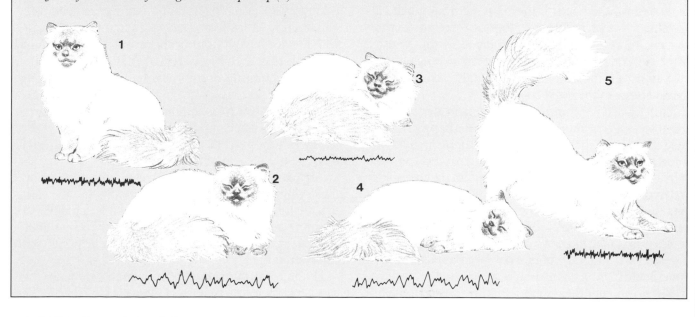

CAN CATS TALK?

Left: *A cat's meow has many modulations, each with its own meaning, from the soft mew of greeting to the more insistent sound that means "feed me". Cats respond to vocal stimulus; the more you talk to your cat the more it will "talk" to you.*

Above: *Purring is a cat's way of expressing pleasure, well-being and affection for its owner. Half-closed eyes are another sign of a contented cat.*

IF, BY TALK, we mean can cats form words in English, French, or some other language, then the answer is no. Cats definitely cannot "talk." But they can make many audible sounds – from purring to meowing to screeching – that they use to communicate with us and with each other.

Experts are not sure where cats produce the sound of purring. Some think it is the sound of turbulence in the main vein of the heart. Others suspect that when cats arch their backs the blood vibrates throughout their bodies, creating sounds that resonate in the sinuses. Most experts, however, think purring is produced by vibrations of membranes, called false vocal cords, located close to the vocal cords.

Purring usually communicates contentment; kittens use it to tell their mothers that they are happy. It is an easy sound for them to produce because it does not interfere with suckling. Approaching mother cats also purr to assure kittens that they are not in danger. Older kittens purr when enticing adults to play. Dominant cats do it when approaching inferior ones in peace or play. And sick animals barely able to defend themselves purr in the hope of soothing potential aggressors, proving that purring should not be taken as a sign of good health.

Meowing, another sound readily associated with cats, is often the call of an abandoned or unhappy kitten – if they are cold, lost, awakened by a returning mother, or in some other way annoyed and malcontent. Adult cats also meow to signal discontent, unhappiness, or need, perhaps even a need for mating. Cats of both sexes use a version of meowing for a mating call.

Gurgling, a high-pitched, friendly greeting, is less common. If combined with gentle meows, it becomes a kind of social contact sound known as "chatting." Although it varies from one cat to another, some cats will do it for half an hour or more and modulate sound so much that they rarely repeat themselves. Another version of gurgling occurs when a mother first brings prey to her kittens. Gurgling can also border on a scream when mum is announcing prey that is larger and possibly dangerous.

Screeching is what cats do when they are in great distress; it is also done just after mating.

Anyone who has ever heard a cat in the night knows the crying sound of a tom cat caterwauling. The call is usually mistaken for a love song, but it is actually a cry of threat and war. Toms rivalling for the same queen are especially known to threaten each other with caterwauling.

Hissing is an audible warning sign that is made when cats expel their breath hard. They expel it so hard when

Right: Cats communicate as much through body language and facial expression as through vocalizations. Male cats locked in combat emit intense yowls and screeches, accompanied by threatening facial expressions: ears flattened, eyes wide open and teeth bared.

Below: When cats communicate with each other they meow much more loudly than they do with humans. Some breeds, such as the Siamese, are more talkative than others.

Below: The vocal apparatus of cats is very different from that of humans. Vocal sounds are produced by changes in the tension of muscles in the throat and mouth, and by changes in the speed of air moving over the vocal cords, which are stretched across the larynx. The vibration of the "false" vocal cords may be involved in purring.

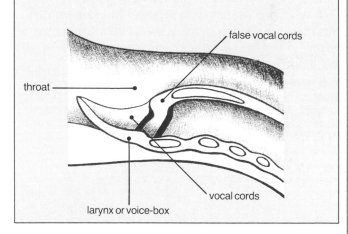

hissing that if one is close enough he or she can feel the air jet. That's why cats shy away if you blow in their faces; even the look of hissing without sounds or air movement can repulse cats.

Growling is an offensive, rather than defensive, sound. Repeated growling turns into snarling.

Tooth-chattering occurs when cats see prey but cannot reach it. Because they want the prey so badly, they move their mouths as if they were in the process of killing.

HOW ELSE DO CATS COMMUNICATE?

BESIDES PRODUCING IDENTIFIABLE sounds, cats also communicate in other nonvocal ways: body language, touch and scent. Cats' body language consists of a wide variety of postures and movements involving just about any part of the body, from the eyes and ears to the tail and the hair.

Ears pointed forward convey friendly interest and attentiveness or suspense. Ears pricked and slightly back warn that attack is coming. Ears back and sideways signal defensiveness, fear, and readiness to flee. Flattened ears suggest fear or submission. When hunting, ears are drawn back, contributing to a watchful appearance. A contented cat sits with its eyes half closed and ears upright.

Erect ears communicate annoyance, and eyes are likely to be narrowed to a vertical slit. Narrowed pupils are a sign of tension, heightened interest, and aggressive threat, whereas dilated pupils express surprise, fear, and defensiveness. Since the size of pupils also depends on incoming light, moods cannot be gauged by eyes alone.

In moods of excitement and fearfulness, cheek muscles pull the cheek ruff down towards the throat, sometimes in pulsing rhythm. Whiskers, if pointed forward and fanned, indicate tension and attentiveness; if sideways and less fanned, calmness and comfort; if bunched and flattened, shyness.

Yawning expresses reassurance and contentment. Spitting is a sudden gesture used when frightened or angry, often accompanied by forepaws hitting the ground, arching of the back, and raising of the fur along the spine. Although no attack usually occurs, cats achieve their purpose of threatening or warning just by using the bluffing gesture.

The position of the head conveys messages, too. Stretched forward, it means readiness for contact; if raised it means dominance; when lowered, inferiority; and when lowered jerkily with chin pulled in or turned sideways, it means lack of interest.

Legs stretched to full length show self-confidence or readiness for attack. Bent hind legs signify uncertainty or timidity; bent forelegs, desire to avoid conflict but willingness to defend if necessary; all legs bent, uncertainty, caution, or defensiveness.

A stretched-out body belongs to a confident or ready-to-attack cat. A constricted or arched back displays fear and defensiveness. When ready to mate, queens crouch in a position known as lordosis.

Quick, side-to-side tail movements indicate excitement. Rapid waving is an expression of annoyance. A still, raised tail is a friendly greeting and an invitation to sniff the anal region. An upright tail twitching slightly belongs to an alert cat. A tail that whips up suddenly is a threat of attack.

Mutual grooming reinforces the bond between two cats. When one seemingly clean cat does it alone, it may feel threatened or stressed. Cats also rub noses and rub against their owners and each other to signify acceptance and submission.

War Games
Right: Cats may fight over territory, or a mate, but actual combat is always a last resort. More often, a ritual display of aggression is enough to see off an opponent. The combatants first investigate each other by sniffing at scent glands on the face (1). Swishing his tail, the aggressor sniffs the base of the opponent's tail and gives a threatening growl, putting the second cat on the defensive. The aggressor is now poised to strike (2) and the defensive cat crouches low, with ears and tail flat. The confrontation may end here, with the loser adopting a defensive posture and backing off (3). In this case the aggressor walks off disdainfully, leaving the loser to slink away. However, if the aggressor's challenge is met, fighting will ensue. *The defendant first adopts the defensive threat, turning its body sideways and arching its back to look more imposing. The tail bristles and curls up (4). The aggressor, unimpressed, keeps on coming (5). The defendant crouches low, presses its ears flat to its head and hisses at its opponent. The pussyfooting is over (6). The aggressor pounces and the second cat defends itself by kicking out with its legs, claws out. The battle continues until the loser spots a chance to escape with as much dignity as it can muster.*

1

2

Left: *If a cat is frightened, its hair stands up evenly all over. When a cat is threatening, its hair stands up only in a band along the spine and on the tail. In attack, hair stands up and also inclines toward the middle, forming a ridge.*

Above: *Perky ears and relaxed whiskers mark the face of a happy cat (1). An angered cat will push back its erect ears, narrow its pupils to slits, and push its whiskers forward (2). Flattened ears and whiskers and widened pupils show that a cat is frightened (3). A cat opens its pupils, perks up its ears, and bristles its whiskers forward when hunting and playing (4). A cat that is in ecstasy when being patted or when satisfied relaxes its eyes and whiskers (5).*

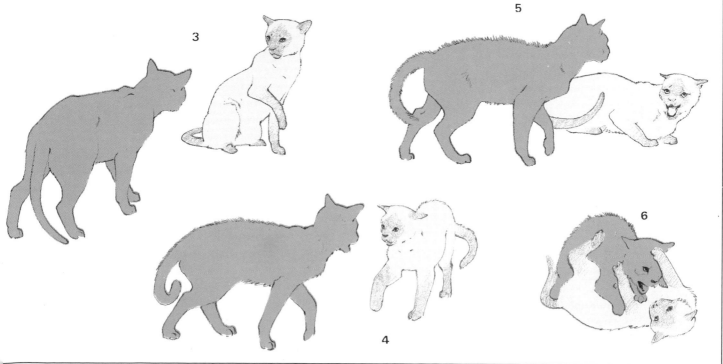

DO CATS HAVE INSTINCTS?

ALTHOUGH KITTENS LEARN some behaviour by watching older cats, many reactions, especially those related to survival, are instinctive. For example, kittens will respond to certain stimuli even before their eyes are open. If disturbed, they may hiss or spit. They are also born knowing how to suckle; if they didn't, they would not be able to eat and would soon die.

Another natural habit is for kittens to rest next to their siblings; this provides both warmth and security. House cats can also produce normal cat sounds without hearing them first. Even kittens born deaf develop their species' normal repertoire. Cats all seem to be born with a passion for curiosity and wandering, and during adventures they develop enough sense to know the possibility of danger and to land on their feet during a fall.

Sexual desires and reactions are instinctive and not learned. When the time comes for queens to become mothers, instinct drives them to look for a partner and get impregnated.

The mother cat instinctively knows how to give birth to and care for the kittens until the kittens are able to care for themselves. Sometimes, after several weeks, when the kittens no longer need quite so much physical protection, she obeys an instinct which tells her to move the nest to a less confined space.

It is unlikely that cats learn these things by watching other cats, because in most cases there are no other cats around to observe. But there are some things that cats do have to learn. Although kittens are born with the instinct not to dirty their own nest, they do not know exactly where to relieve themselves unless they are shown. And even though they appear to know how to bury their faeces to protect themselves from predators, it is more likely that they learn this habit by watching other cats. Experiments have demonstrated that cats not shown how to hunt by other cats do not develop skills for killing hunted prey. Most cats who know how to hunt and kill prey have learned this by watching their mothers.

Some experts believe that some of these instincts have been bred out of cats, that years and years of domesticating cats has changed them into more home-like, companionable animals, quite different from the wild cats that formerly roamed the planet. After all, being a pet and having food, litter box, warmth, amusement, and security provided is much easier than living on your own in the wild. Human intervention which they experience early in their lives gives whatever wild instincts today's house cats have little chance to develop very far.

Right: The ritual of courtship may be prolonged, though the sex act itself is very brief. (1) The female signals her willingness to mate by calling and displaying to the male as he circles her. (2) The male mounts her, grabbing the scruff of her neck. (3) He arches his back to achieve penetration, and ejaculates after one or two pelvic thrusts. (4) At the moment of ejaculation, the female emits a loud piercing cry and turns upon the bemused male. The whole procedure may be repeated subsequently, however.

Left: When a cat is brought up with other animals – even rabbits, which are normally considered "fair game" – the hunting instinct seems not to come to the fore.

Below: The predator instinct exists to some extent in all cats, including those that lead well-fed, cossetted lives in a comfortable family home.

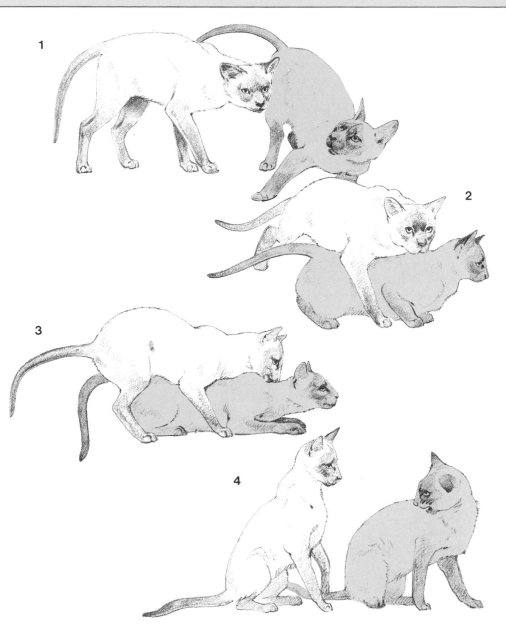

CAT WATCHING TIP

All cats hunt. Can yours kill? The answer to this question will tell you something about your cat's recent ancestry. Hunting mothers generally pass all their hunting abilities, including the ultimate killing of their prey, onto their kittens. Nonhunting mothers, by contrast, often pass along the hunting skills except the ability to kill. A cat's tendency to hunt or not to hunt will have been determined by its ancestors of several generations ago.

DO CATS HAVE A SIXTH SENSE?

IT'S A QUIET evening. There doesn't seem to be anything moving or making a sound for miles. You're calm and at peace. Yet, there is your cat, hackles raised (ears back, pupils dilated, back arched, fur standing up, tail twitching, hissing), staring intently into the direction of…well, nothing. Or maybe, from complete stillness, it suddenly makes a mad dash through the house at top speed, flinging itself at…again, nothing.

It's behaviour like this that makes people think that cats have a sixth sense – ESP (extra-sensory perception) or some sort of spiritual awareness that they alone possess. Their natural aloofness feeds into this theory, as they always seem to be one step ahead of us, to know more about some things than we do.

Cats behave like electronic security systems – sometimes even like spiritual mediums – because the senses they have are so finely tuned. When a cat becomes alarmed in an apparently safe situation, it is reacting to sounds or vibrations we can't detect. When it, for example, clears out of a building before an earthquake or volcanic eruption, it has detected pre-disaster changes in the environment. Or, more simply, it hears the sounds or detects the smells of other animals in the vicinity – signals not meant for humans.

So, it is not ESP that makes cats behave so mysteriously at times. What, then, of their age-old connection with evil and bad luck?

During medieval times, cats were linked with witches and black magic; they were thought to be

Below: During the Middle Ages, cats suffered terrible persecution at the hands of superstitious people who believed that witches could change themselves into cats and back again at will. So many cats were burned alive that the species was almost extinct in Europe in 1400. These witches are depicted accompanied by a cat, a dog, a mouse and an owl – their "familiars", or demons in the form of animals.

Right: Mad, bad and dangerous to know? Some people are actually repelled by cats, regarding them as "spooky". Certainly the cat is an aloof creature of independent spirit, and this may help to explain the magical or diabolical nature so long attributed to it.

Right: Although cats seem to display a special "sixth sense" at times, most of the "extra-sensory powers" attributed to cats are simply due to their extremely well-developed senses. Natural hunters, cats are equipped with super-sensitive hearing, keen eyesight and a strong sense of smell, so it is not surprising that they can sense approaching rain before we do, or hear sounds inaudible to the human ear.

Below: Contrary to the old wives' tale, cats do not deliberately attempt to smother babies. They are, however, curious about every new addition – human or otherwise – to their household.

witches' familiars or even forms of the witches themselves. After all, they travelled at night, sometimes caterwauling, giving rise to tales of evil orgies. They bonded with elderly, solitary childless women who were perhaps vulnerable to the accusation of being witches by superstitious and ignorant neighbours. Such a superstition might be given some substance by the fact that there are cats who dislike men (for reasons of some previous negative experience with men or an aversion to deep voices). Cats were considered evil by the Christian church, which decried the ancient Egyptians' belief that they were sacred. And cats' refusal to be subservient like other domestic animals fed the belief that they were sinister in some way. It was believed that parts of the cat's body were dangerous to body and soul: their teeth were venomous, their flesh poisonous, their hair lethal (causing suffocation), and breath infectious (causing consumption).

Even today, some people still subscribe to the old wives' tale that a cat will try to smother a new baby in the house. And even if they don't really believe in the omen, people in America and other countries may consider it bad luck when a black cat crosses their path or enters their house. Conversely, in Great Britain, black cats are thought to bring good fortune.

CAT WATCHING TIP

The next time your cat raises its hackles in an apparently quiet house, check more closely for the noise you didn't hear. Because cats' senses are so much more attuned than humans', it's likely that your cat actually has felt, seen, smelled or heard something that interests it.

Have a check round. Your cat's whiskers may have felt a slight draught, maybe from a small crack in your walls that you've never noticed. Maybe it saw movement, something fast and minute. Maybe it smelled another cat or some other creature outside, somewhere on its territory. Or maybe its ears picked up a high-pitched noise from the animal kingdom.

DO CATS LOVE?

THERE IS NO proof that cats love like humans do. But despite a reputation for being aloof, cats often seek out their owners and each other and respond in kind to affection and attention. If not loving, cats are at the very least sociable animals, even if it's because they know that such sociability works to their advantage.

Their first "loving" contact occurs just after birth, when their mother cleans them with her tongue and provides them with milk. Kittens tend to feel affectionate towards the mother in response to her caring. This positive contact carries over into their adult lives, when humans provide for them in some of the same ways that their mothers did.

Cats express this affection by rubbing their muzzles and bodies against the owner's legs, licking a hand or face, or lying on their backs inviting an affectionate pat or stroke. Some experts say that the only reason cats do this is to exchange scents, a normal part of a friendly greeting. Yet, as if remembering how it felt when licked by mother or snuggling with littermates, cats may close their eyes from the pleasure of this type of physical contact with people.

Cats sometimes show affection for their owners by bringing back killed prey as a gift, just as a mother does for her kittens. However, some say cats do this because they think their owners are unskilled hunters (like kittens) and need to be fed or taught to kill prey!

Unlike dogs, cats don't consider themselves "owned." People would do better to look upon cats as roommates who choose to spend their time with them for the fulfilment of mutual goals. A cat's affection has to be won. Unlike a dog, a cat won't, out of loyalty or pack instinct, remain where it has been mistreated. But it will bond to an understanding, appreciative owner and respond with affection and respect. Cats also demonstrate what might be called affection with other cats. Females sometimes help other cats who are giving birth and take part in caring for the kittens.

Left: Strong bonds of affection develop between the cat and its human family. Research has shown that owning a pet can reduce stress levels and the risk of heart attack in humans.

Above: Spoils of the kill. Much to the consternation of their owners, some cats will bring back dead or half-dead prey as a "gift". This may be a sign of affection, or more often it may simply be the compensatory behaviour of would-be mothers.

Left: The female cat is a devoted mother, lavishing attention on her brood and patiently indulging them in their boisterous games.

Right: Some cats become quite attached to an individual member of the family and insist on spending a great deal of time and affection on them.

WHY DO CATS PLAY?

PLAY IN CATS is a lot like play in humans. It's fun for the kids (kittens), and that's why they do it. But it also serves as a learning experience for them, teaching them the basic skills they need to survive into adulthood. Most mammals experience play as part of their maturation, and those who don't become social misfits and poor hunters. Kittens start to play when they are about three weeks old with general rough-and-tumble actions. They jump each other, roll over, and grapple. At this stage, nobody gets hurt because nobody has the strength to hurt.

Play becomes more elaborate a few weeks later. They chase, pounce, grab with their front paws, kick with hind legs, and add some hunting manoeuvres:

The "mouse pounce" consists of hiding, crouching, creeping, running towards and jumping on some object of prey.

The "bird swat" begins with the same approach, but ends with a leap and blow with one of the front feet to a hanging or midair object.

The "fish scoop" is used when the prey is on the ground. The paw is flung out, and the object is scooped up and batted over the head or shoulder.

Perhaps because kittens are uncoordinated in comparison to cats, or because they appear to be just huge heads and wide eyes surrounded by fur at this stage, every move they make seems very cute, exaggerated, and unnecessary, giving off an air of fun for the sake of fun.

Above left: Some cats and dogs get along quite well, and many become inseparable companions, particularly if they have been brought up together from an early age.

Above right: Plants hold a special fascination, and in some instances danger, for kittens. Make sure that any poisonous plants are kept well out of the way.

Kittens' vigour for play declines at the age of five months. Experts have surmised that it is because, in the wild, kittens would be out on their own at about that time. Or perhaps because they have learned all the right moves by then and are quite capable of being serious about what they have learned.

But like Peter Pan, who never grew up, domestic cats never mature in the sense that they need to know how to hunt or provide for their own survival – their owners provide for them like parents – so most house cats, although physically and sexually mature, will still enjoy what we would call playing. Pet stores sell a variety of squeaky, chewable, rollable, ringable toys for cats' amusement long after their formative months have passed. These, and a lot of normal household objects – string, balls of wool, feathers, rolled-up paper – or another cat or pet can keep a cat amused for hours on end with a little enticement, and sometimes even without that enticement.

Below: Despite their reputation for being aloof, cats are highly social animals. Acquaintances will often engage in mock fights, just as kittens do.

Left: Rough-and-tumble play among littermates helps the kittens acquire some of the essential skills they need in later life. At six to eight weeks old, they engage in mock fights which involve mutual chasing, swatting, wrestling, grappling and neck-biting, all carried out in a spirit of fun.

CAT WATCHING TIP

Play remains an integral part of life for many cats, even well into their later years. Kittens, of course, are the most active and persistent in their activities, but nearly every cat, even the most sedate, will play from time to time. What is your cat's play quotient?

WHY DO CATS ESTABLISH TERRITORIES?

Above: *Lord of all he surveys. Ideally a cat's territory will include a high point from which it can keep an eye on things. The dominant tom does not tolerate competition from other cats within his territory.*

CAT MYTH

Cats want to die alone.

Many romanticize what they say is the cats' need to die alone – without being affected by humans, completely in the wild, joined with the Earth. The truth is that cats don't even know about death. They can hardly anticipate what they don't know about.

What they do know is that they are being threatened (by illness or injury). But they cannot see this predator, so instinct tells them to hide where the predator cannot find them. Unfortunately, they take this "predator" with them when they hide, and they may die alone, without help or comfort from those who love them.

CATS ESTABLISH TERRITORIES for much the same reasons that humans build or buy homes – to have a safe place of their own for sleeping, eating, defecating and recreation. Like humans, cats are territorial by nature. Even house cats who never go outside have favourite places within the house for their needs, even if it's only a room or a part of a chair. Where several cats live in a house, territories may blur until all residents jointly claim the house and offer mutual defence against others. If your cat is not confined indoors, it will also have a territory outside the house and a social position to go along with it.

Humans have made it easy, in some cases, for cats to choose territories. Fences, pavements, driveways, gardens and shrubbery have set up boundaries that can be easily followed if there are a lot of cats in the area. Sometimes humans assist in designating boundaries by chasing other cats away or breaking up fights.

Cats mark their territories by scratching and depositing scents in their urine and faeces or from glands on their bodies. Territories can be as large as 100 acres or more for rural cats and as small as a few feet for house or city cats. In households with more than one cat, territories are sometimes time-shared: one cat gets it in the morning, another in the afternoon.

Cats organize themselves into family-type hierarchies in which every cat has a position and follows certain rules. New cats in the neighbourhood must fight to be accepted and win territory. Males are organized by strength. The toughest tom becomes the head of the "family", with power over the other members in the ranks below him. Occasional changes occur in position when one member is overthrown or neutered. Although tom cats rule the biggest area of territory, they do not get priority in courtship. Land, not sex, is what puts them at the top.

Females are organized by their motherly accomplishments. The queen with the most kittens is top mama. When queens are neutered, they slide down on the social ladder. Females and neutered males possess only small plots and fight harder than big tom cats to retain their little islands. Cats who own large areas are not as possessive because they have so much territory and are unable to spend enough time protecting it all. But when they decide to fight, they usually win.

Amid the private properties there are common grounds for socializing, mating, hunting, or whatever. To reach these places, cats have to follow certain trails so as not to violate other territories or antagonize enemies (like dogs). Some paths are private, but most are common, like human roads.

Right: The extent of a cat's territory depends on its position in the hierachy. Queens with kittens (far right) have small territories which they defend fiercely. A tom (left) will probably have the most extensive area. All cats will avoid gardens where there is a dog, but some areas, such as paths, will be communal.

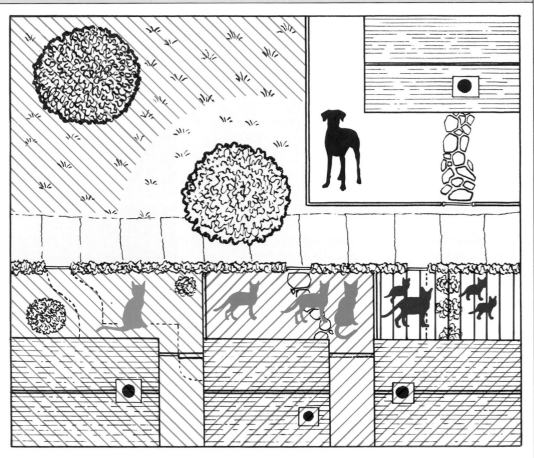

Left: Cats use scent marks to indicate territorial limits and to leave behind information for other cats about the status, sex and route of the depositor. Tom cats spray their boundaries with pungent urine. More subtle marks are left by rubbing the chin, forehead and tail against doorways, trees and fences; this action deposits scent from the sebaceous glands.

CAT WATCHING TIP

You may not think your cat has a territory, but all cats do in some form. Follow your cat out into the garden. Make note of where it goes, what it looks at, what it marks, and how it reacts to other creatures in its proximity. Notice where it settles down and what paths it takes to get to where it wants to be. Note if there is also a common ground where it meets up with other cats, and what kind of social standing your cat seems to have as a member of the group. Do this for several days because the cat might not cover all its territory in just one.

DO CATS SEE IN COLOUR?

PEOPLE USED TO think that cats were colour-blind and could see only in black and white. This belief came about because cats did not and apparently could not be taught to respond to other colours.

Recently, however, cats have been taught to distinguish between colours: red from green, red from blue, red from grey, green from blue, green from grey, blue from grey, yellow from blue, and yellow from grey. Cats don't seem to think much of this ability and, in fact, don't need to know one colour from another. Cats' eyes are highly developed in other areas, accommodating skills that are important to cats.

For example, cats' eyes are very well adapted to dim light. Like in humans, cats' retinas contain two kinds of receptor cells: rods and cones. Rods aid night vision and sensitivity to low light, and cones aid resolution. Cats' eyes contain more rods and fewer cones than those of humans. Therefore they see better at night, but the image is somewhat fuzzy.

Cats' eyes also contain a special light-conserving mechanism called the *tapetum lucidum*, which reflects any light not absorbed as it passes through the retina. As a result, the retina gets a second chance to receive the light, aiding cats' night vision even more. This reflective mechanism is also what is responsible for cats' eyes glowing in the dark when light hits them at certain angles.

The night glow occurs when the pupil is at its widest, in very dim light. But cats' pupils protect the eyes from very bright light, too, by contracting to just narrow slits. When the pupils are contracted to their maximum, they close completely in the middle and are still open to the size of pinholes at the tops and bottoms. Light that is too bright to be handled by the narrowing of the pupils can be accommodated by cats' shutting their eyes.

Cats also have binocular vision, meaning that parts of the field of each eye overlap. This skill is necessary for three-dimensional vision, which is necessary for hunting animals. Without it, cats could not judge distance, depth or size. Because binocular vision is not as pronounced in some breeds, such as the Siamese, they are not as successful hunters. Cats' eyes are also very sensitive to movements, another plus for felines that hunt.

But, even with all these ocular abilities, a cat is not born with the ability to use them. Kittens are born blind and, at eight to 20 days, when the eyes open, they have to "learn" how to handle all the stimuli coming in through their eyes. They are unlikely to master the organs until they are approximately 12 weeks old.

Above: The cat's pupil varies dramatically in shape and size according to the intensity of the light. In bright daylight it shrinks to become a mere slit. In poor light the pupil dilates, until it fills almost the whole diameter of the iris, to collect the maximum amount of light.

Left: The stare of the cat. Deep and luminous, cats' eyes have a mysterious power. The Ancient Egyptian word for cat was "mau", which means "to see".

Above: The Siamese gene causes abnormal nerve connections between the eyes and the brain resulting in poor binocular (three-dimensional) vision. Some cats develop a squint apparently in an effort to compensate for this.

CAT WATCHING TIP

Maybe the results won't contribute to the advancement of scientific understanding of the cat, but you can do a little experiment to demonstrate your cat's colour vision.

Set up three boxes the same size but of different colours – red, green and blue. Place some of your cat's favourite food in the red one, showing your cat that it's there, and help it get to it. Repeat this process several times over several days, always keeping the boxes in the same location relative to one another. After a week or so, switch the red box with one of the others and put the food in the red box. Which box does your cat go to?

That is also about the time their eyes change to their permanent colour. The most common shades are orange, yellow, hazel, green and blue. Many white cats with blue eyes are born deaf, and in cats with one blue eye, the corresponding ear is partially deaf. No matter what the colour of the iris, with rare exception the pupil is usually black.

HOW DEVELOPED ARE CATS' SENSES?

CATS ARE ESSENTIALLY walking sensory organs, with just about every part of their bodies involved in taking in stimuli from their environments. Their tongues alone are involved in three of the main senses. Cats' sense of smell is good, in fact, because they not only have their nose to smell with, they also have an additional sense organ – the Jacobson's organ – in the upper surface of the mouth. Scents are picked up from the air on the tongue as it is pressed against the Jacobson's organ and passed along to the brain. Cats are among many carnivores that make a strange lip-curling, nose-wrinkling grimace, called flehming, thought to bring the chemicals of some odours, probably sexual ones, in contact with the Jacobson's organ.

Their noses are particularly sensitive to odours that contain nitrogen, enabling cats to reject rancid odours that contain this element. Cats are also very sensitive to heavily chlorinated tap water.

Cats perceive good odours, too, as anyone who has ever watched a cat with a catnip toy knows. Cats almost make love to the herb and in its presence act in the same way that toms act around females in heat. Catnip contains a chemical called trans-neptalactone, which resembles a substance excreted by females in their urine. The herb valerian can also evoke this response.

Kittens are born with a good sense of taste, but it diminishes as they age. That is why cats sometimes show little interest in their food, gaining a reputation for finickiness. The taste buds are present on the tip, sides and base of the tongue, but none of them is sensitive to sweet-tasting foods.

Cats' tongues are versatile muscles. They are able to form a ladle for lapping up water, and they contain rough sections called papillae for holding prey and for grooming. They are also just as sensitive as the skin on the nose and the pads of the paws because they contain sensitive nerve endings.

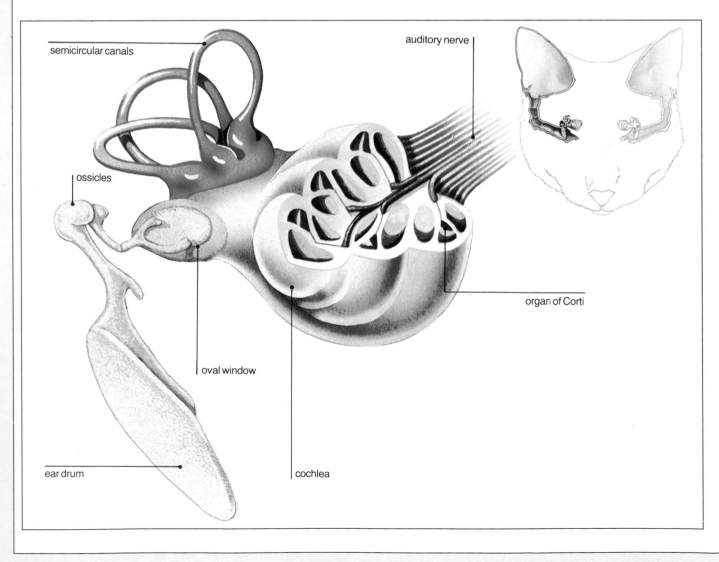

semicircular canals

auditory nerve

ossicles

organ of Corti

oval window

ear drum

cochlea

The senses of smell and taste are closely linked in the cat, since the nasal passage opens into the mouth. Receptors in the olfactory mucosa send signals to the olfactory lobe of the brain. Molecules of a scent are picked up from the air on the tongue, which is then pressed against the Jacobson's organ, located in the upper surface of the mouth, which sends signals to centres in the hypothalamic region of the brain concerned with appetite and sexual behaviour.

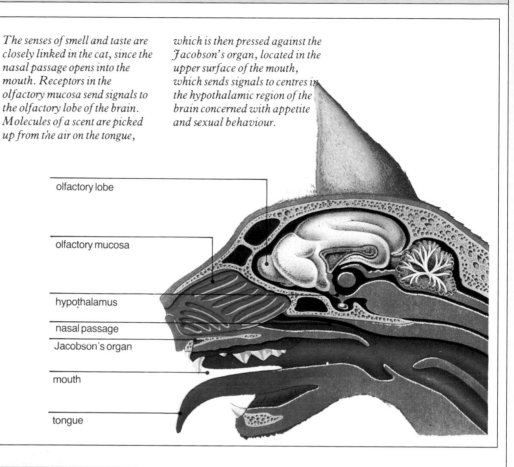

olfactory lobe

olfactory mucosa

hypothalamus

nasal passage

Jacobson's organ

mouth

tongue

Above: *With all his senses alert, this cat is exploring his environment.*

Below: *Cats' whiskers are highly sensitive "antennae", and can detect the slightest touch or pressure.*

The hair follicles, including the whiskers, are able to detect the slightest movement, and cats travelling at night, and those with poor vision, use them to negotiate their steps. Cats' ears are equipped with more than a dozen muscles that enable them to move towards sounds. They can perceive high-frequency sounds up to about 65 kHz (65 kilohertz, or 65,000 cycles per second). In comparison, human ears have a capacity up to 20 kHz. As in humans, cats' sensitivity to high notes reduces with age, beginning as early as three years of age and being very obvious by age four or five.

CAT WATCHING TIP

Has your cat ever curled its upper lip back as though it were attempting to dislodge a food particle from between its teeth? At the same time, you may have noticed that it was quite erect and alert. This is an action known as flehming. With it, the cat is drawing odours to an organ on the roof of its mouth, an additional "smelling" apparatus.

SELECTING A CAT

BEFORE YOU TAKE home a cat, you need to consider the animal's care, breeding, origin, gender, age, temperament and health. To help you decide on a feline companion, ask yourself these questions:

● Do you have a lifestyle conducive to pet ownership? (If your job involves considerable travel and would result in the cat being alone much of the time, your lifestyle is not the best for a cat.) Do you have room enough for a cat's necessities? And do you have time and money to feed it, groom it, exercise it, train it and take it to the vet for regular checkups?

● Do you want a pedigreed or nonpedigreed animal? If you are interested in showing or breeding, you will need a pedigree cat. If this is your reason for getting a cat, you should take along an expert in breeds. Pedigreed cats are expensive, reflecting the effort that has been put into building up a bloodline, but it may be possible to strike a deal with the breeder, perhaps by taking a "flawed" cat – one that is ineligible for show – or maybe by offering to return the cat periodically for breeding. If you are interested more in companionship, you might as well get a nonpedigreed cat.

● Where should you get your cat? If you are buying a pedigree, get it from a specialist breeder, preferably one that is recommended by a local cat club. An animal shelter and another cat owner are good places to find mongrels ("moggie" or "alley cat"). Avoid pet shops if possible because conditions there sometimes promote disease. Try to observe the cat with its littermates or in its natural surroundings so you can see how it has been treated.

● Do you want a male or a female? Either sex makes a good companion, but there are certain habits associated with each gender. An unneutered tom (male) cat, for example, will spray and fight more than a neutered male. An unneutered queen (female) will have periods of oestrus (in heat, every three weeks) and possibly unwanted pregnancies. Neutered cats are generally more affectionate and do not contribute to the population of unwanted animals constantly surrendered to animal shelters for euthanasia.

● Do you want a kitten or an adult? Kittens demand lots of attention and need to be trained, but they adapt better than an adult to a new home. If

you work, you may want to consider a trained adult. Training a kitten is very difficult unless you can be consistent. If you bring home an adult, keep it in the house for a few days so it does not try to return to its previous home.

● Does the cat have a good temperament? It should be alert, friendly and willing to be handled.

● Is the cat healthy? When buying a cat it is a wise idea to take the cat along to your vet for an examination and obtain a certificate of health. A humane society will have already given a kitten its vaccinations, and even its boosters if it is an adult. The cat should also have a blood test for feline leukaemia, which is transmittable to other cats. You might also want to do an informal check of your own on the cat's eyes, ears, mouth, anus area and coat.

Left: As cute and as perfect as the kitten may seem, selection of a cat should be based on more than simple emotion. Owning a cat is a long-term responsibility – anything up to 20 years – so it is important to be sure you can give your pet the care and attention it needs.

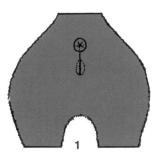

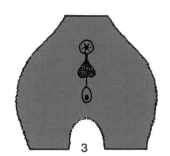

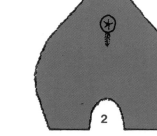

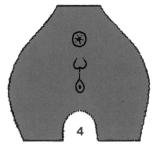

Left: Sexing cats and kittens. In the male and the female there are two openings – that closest to the tail being the anus – but they are much closer together in the female than the male. (1) Adult female: space between anus and vulva about ½in (1cm). (2) Female kitten: anus and vulva are very close together. Vulva appears as a distinct slit. (3) Adult male: anal and genital openings are about 1in (2.5cm) apart. Testicles clearly visible in entire tom. (4) Male kitten: tip of penis is hidden in a small round opening about ½in (1cm) below the anus. In between, the scrotal sacs appear as raised darkish areas. Testicles not obvious until about six weeks.

Below: The appeal of cats as pets lies in their ability to give love, companionship, loyalty and amusement, while retaining an admirable independence and self-sufficiency.

CAT MYTH

Cats interfere when you talk on the telephone because they are jealous.

We've all had it happen to us a few times. You're sitting quietly in a room with another person who suddenly starts talking, sometimes looking off into the distance, sometimes looking at you.

You don't see anyone else in the room so you respond to what she is saying. And then, through some look on her face or some change in her position, you realize that she wasn't talking to you, but to someone on the phone. Only you didn't realize because the phone cord was hidden under her hair or behind her head.

You have an advantage over cats. You know what a phone is and what it means when you see someone is using one. A cat, however, knows only that someone in the room is talking and that no one else is around, so the person must be talking to it. Instead of being jealous, it is doing what it normally does when someone talks with it; it moves in close to respond, with a rub or a nuzzle.

GETTING READY FOR YOUR NEW CAT

FIRST, MAKE SURE your house is safe for the cat. Get rid of toxic plants (including rhododendrons, azaleas, poinsettias and oleander), hide rubbish bins, put a barrier on your cooker and in front of your fireplace, shut cupboard doors, lock doors to high balconies, manoeuvre electrical cords out of the cat's reach, and put away ornaments, decorations, sharp or small objects, plastic bags, irons, or other items that could injure the cat. (Also, make sure that other animals and infants are safe from the cat. Wire mesh can be placed over fish bowls and cots until you are sure your cat considers these beings part of the family.)

You'll need to buy some essentials, including a cat bed, a litter box and dishes for food and water. Beds come in anything from cardboard (which cannot be cleaned), to wicker (which may be draughty), to plastic (which is easy to clean), to quilted cotton (which is comfortable and washable). Place the bed in a secluded, warm place free from draughts, maybe near the boiler if it is a fairly safe, clean area. Position the food and water bowls near the bed and make the litter box accessible but not too close to the other areas and not in the lane of household traffic. Keep these items clean; wash them separately from other dishware.

Some of the extras you might also like to obtain are grooming tools, a carrying container, a collar with a name tag (if your cat will be allowed outside), a scratching post or pad, a cat flap for the outside door, and cat toys. An adult cat may feel more comfortable with a toy of its own, and a young or ill cat may like a heating pad or hot water bottle under part of its bed.

When you first bring kitty home, keep children and other pets away from it until it has had time to explore its new area, one room at a time, without interference. Then confine it to its own room until it becomes accustomed to it. Introduce the cat to other members of the household individually. With other animals, give

Right: A new cat or kitten should be kept indoors for at least a few days so that it has time to get to know its new home. The first trips outdoors should be supervised, otherwise the cat might wander off or take fright and bolt. Make sure all garden weedkillers and pesticides are kept locked away.

Below: In view of a cat's inquisitive nature and its proficiency in climbing, it is a wise precaution to keep ornaments and valuables out of reach if possible.

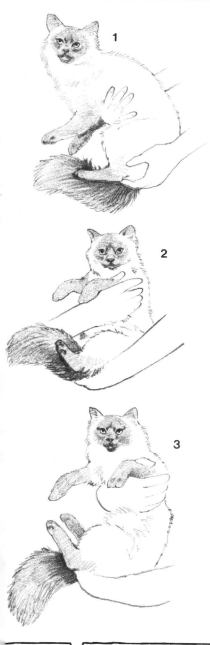

Left: *The correct way to pick up a cat. (1) Place one hand under its front legs and the other under the hind quarters. (2) Keep one hand firmly under the hind quarters, supporting the cat's full weight. (3) Hold the cat upright, with one hand round its upper chest for support.*

Below: *To maintain a safe environment for your pet, watch out for potential hazards around the home, such as: (1) pans of boiling water or fat; (2) open oven doors; (3) rubbish bins harbouring bacteria and small fish bones; (4) boiling kettles; (5) sharp utensils; (6) household detergents; (7) open fridges; (8) open dryers or washing machines; (9) sockets and electrical cables which the cat may chew; (10) open doors leading onto high balconies; (11) objects resting on table edges; (12) precarious ornaments on shelves; (13) fires with no fireguards; (14) poisonous houseplants; (15) drawers left open where the cat may become trapped; (16) young children or babies left alone in a room with a cat.*

CAT MYTH

Cats sulk after being scolded.
We think a lot of our cats. So when we have to reprimand them, we feel that we have wounded their pride, stopped them in their confident tracks and caused them to sulk. But all we have really done is intimidate the cat into feeling inferior. When we reprimand, we stare at the cat. Its natural response is to turn away to avoid the hostility.

This makes the cat less afraid and also keeps the cat from staring back, which would be a way of provoking you more and possibly resulting in an attack. So, in a sense, your cat has surrendered.

both affection; don't neglect the old pet for the new. The animals will eventually work out their territories and relationships, so it's not advisable to rush them.

Feed the cat at regular times, change its litter daily, play with it and talk to it, groom it regularly, and schedule it for neutering, regular checkups and booster vaccinations.

As soon as the cat becomes familiar, begin training it to accept your established routines. During your cat's first week in the new home, handle and fuss over it as much as possible before you let it out. When you allow it outdoors, accompany it a few times. Don't allow it out in inclement weather and don't let it roam at night.

GIVING YOUR CAT A PROPER DIET

ALTHOUGH THEY ARE domesticated, cats are carnivores. This means they eat meat and have very little need for other foods. When cats eat their prey, they eat muscle, skin, bones and internal organs. It's your job as a cat owner to try to duplicate that diet. And that means a lot of protein and fat. A good cat diet should contain 25 to 30 percent protein and 15 to 40 percent fat.

·Most cats do very well living on the prepared cat foods on the market. Canned meat foods store easily and have lots of water in them, which is essential for a cat's diet. Soft, moist cat foods are also good. But dried foods are suspected of causing bladder ·problems because they do not contain enough water, so if you use them be sure to provide plenty of fresh water.·

To avoid monotony and maintain balance, some cats also enjoy fresh foods like cooked meat such as poultry, beef, lamb, pork and rabbit. Cooked fish and cheese are also good. (Never give cats raw meat; it could cause toxoplasmosis.)·

Because of the construction of their teeth, cats don't chew; so chop up food or serve in lumps that they can tear up. And make sure there are no bones in the meat.

Some cats may even take vegetables and fruits on occasion, but cats cannot live on vegetarian diets alone.

You may sometimes see your cat eat ordinary grass. Don't be alarmed. Grass is food for cats, acting as an emetic to make them regurgitate furballs and other unwanted matter. If your cat regularly eats grass, be sure your lawn-care products are nontoxic.

Other don'ts involved in feeding a cat:

- Don't feed only liver; it can upset the bowels.

- Don't feed only fish; it can cause vitamin B_1 deficiency.

- Don't feed only prime lean meat; it produces calcium and vitamin deficiencies.

- Don't worry about how much water your cat is getting, as long as you regularly supply fresh water and moist food; some cats don't drink at all in front of their owners but do drink from baths or puddles.

- Don't give water directly from the tap; the strong chlorine odour irritates the sensitive feline nose. Let tap water sit for 24 hours before serving it to a cat.

- Except for a few breeds, as noted later, don't worry about extra vitamin and mineral supplements, so long as your cat is getting a balanced diet.

- Don't give cats raw egg white; it contains avidin, which neutralizes biotin.

- Don't give cats prepared dog food; the meat protein content is not high enough.

CAT MYTH

Well-fed cats are poor hunters.
Cats were originally wild animals. But through centuries of domestication, we have taken them into our homes, cared for them, and removed their need to perform certain activities. In fact, we have made cats somewhat like Peter Pan – they never grow up; we've made it so easy for them that they don't need to.

A cat is either a hunter or not. Kittens that are born of mothers that hunted are probably trained to hunt by their mothers, so long as they are not taken away from them when very young. Kittens that are born of mothers that did not hunt or kittens that are taken away from their hunting mothers before they can learn from them grow up not having learned to hunt. Even if they have something of a stalking instinct, they never really learn to carry it out unless taught by another cat.

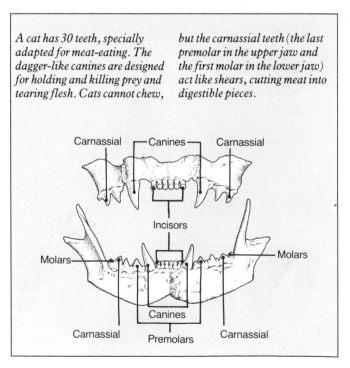

A cat has 30 teeth, specially adapted for meat-eating. The dagger-like canines are designed for holding and killing prey and tearing flesh. Cats cannot chew, but the carnassial teeth (the last premolar in the upper jaw and the first molar in the lower jaw) act like shears, cutting meat into digestible pieces.

Carnassial — Canines — Carnassial
Incisors
Molars — Molars
Carnassial — Canines — Carnassial
Premolars

Right: This chart is based on the findings of the National Research Council and shows recommended daily amounts of alternative types of food for cats of different ages. Note that the figures given are total daily allowances; if you give one dry meal and one canned, halve the quantities for each meal.

Below: The family that eats together stays together. The most reliable way to meet your cat's nutritional needs is to feed it on a reputable brand of canned cat food. This is formulated and tested to ensure that it provides balanced amounts of protein, fat, vitamins and minerals.

CAT DETAILS		FOOD (grams per cat)			
AGE OF CAT	WEIGHT OF CAT IN KG	FEEDS PER DAY	DRY FOOD	SEMI-MOIST FOOD	CANNED FOOD
KITTEN					
10 weeks	0.4-1.0	4	28-70	32-80	80-200
20 weeks	1.2-2.0	3	43-72	50-84	125-208
30 weeks	1.5-2.7	2	42-76	48-86	120-216
40 weeks	2.2-3.8	2	48-84	57-99	141-243
ADULT					
Active	2.2-4.5	1-2	44-90	48-99	123-252
Inactive	2.2-4.5	1-2	53-108	59-122	150-306
Gestation	2.5-4.0	1-2	70-112	80-128	200-320
Lactation	2.5-4.0	3-4	154-280	176-320	440-800
Neutered cat	2.2-4.5	1	55-75	60-80	250
Old cat (over 10 years)	2.2-4.5	3-4	50-75	55-80	200

CAT MYTH

Cats are finicky.

Throughout current history, cats have been given the reputation of being the fussiest members of the animal kingdom. While it is true that some cats have earned their finicky labels for good reason, the great majority are quite pleased with what they are given to eat.

For those that do not seem to go along with everything that their human companions hand out, perhaps we should consider their individual personalities and histories, or think about their place in the animal world as carnivores. Carnivores are meat-eaters and therefore have little need for carbohydrates. If they turn down a leaf from your Caesar salad, they should not be faulted for wishing it were meat.

A wild cat would not kill a mouse and then eat it alongside a busy roadway. And a domestic cat may just rather say no to that packet of moist chicken than eat in the traffic lane of your kitchen while you are cooking a five-course dinner for 10.

Your domestic cat also may not relish one large meal a day. Instead, it might prefer several mouse-sized meals spread out, much the way its instincts would lead it in the wild. (The average mass-produced cat meal is equivalent to about five mice.)

It's also possible, if your cat loses its appetite for 24 hours or more, that it is going into heat (if female) or being fed elsewhere.

TRAINING YOUR CAT

CAT MYTH

Catgut.
Anyone who has ever heard the term catgut probably thinks the worst of cat-haters. But, in truth, catgut has very little to do with cats. Catgut is a tough cord made from the intestines of certain animals – sheep, pigs and horses – but not cats. It is used mainly for surgical sutures and the strings of musical instruments, tennis rackets and archery bows. The intestines are first cleaned, scraped and cured and then dried and polished before being woven into cords.

When the cords were first used for musical instruments centuries ago, the sound they produced may have been said to sound like the musician was playing the guts of a cat – much like the sound cats make when they are mating or being persecuted, as they were several centuries ago.

Today, with the advent of plastics, there is very little need for any animals' intestines to be used for such products.

YOU AND YOUR cat will have very different ideas about what it should be doing and where it should be doing it. So it's best if you establish a routine from the start.

Litter training is probably the habit that owners consider the most important. You begin the training by putting the kitten in the litter box frequently, especially if it looks ready or has begun to crouch with its tail raised. Never rub the kitten's nose in its mistakes; if you do it will regard that spot as a permanent toilet. Just clean up accident areas (hiding the scent if possible) and lavish praise and/or treats when kitty hits it right.

If your cat refuses to use the litter box, move it to another location. Cats don't like their litter too close to their feeding or sleeping area. Using this knowledge to your advantage, you may want to place food near any accident area to keep the cat from using it again.

All cats should be taught to respond to their own names. Try to make the kitten associate its name with something good. Feeding time is the best time to use this strategy. Call the cat and when it comes, give it its meal. Try this between meals, too, and offer some food titbit as a reward. In a matter of time the cat will come

Left: Waiting to be allowed outdoors, this house cat has learned to use non-vocal communication to get its needs across to its owners.

Right: Cat flaps are convenient, allowing the cat freedom of access to the outdoors. Some models are fitted with a lock that is activated by a small magnet hung on the cat's collar, so that the flap cannot be operated by uninvited cats. Keep the flap raised until the cat has got used to going through it, then reduce the aperture gradually until the cat learns that it can push the flap open with its paw.

to associate coming with the name you call out.

If your cat will be going outside on its own, you might want to teach it to use a door flap. Many cats learn this by themselves, simply by employing their own curiosity. If yours doesn't, you'll want to show it some of the things that await it in the world outside.

Make sure the flap is firmly open before you start. Then let the cat investigate. To get it to go through, place some food on the other side. After it is through, release the flap and use food to entice it back into the house. If necessary, show it that pushing will open the flap.

Some cats also need negative training to keep them from biting, jumping, scratching, relaxing on your bed, or whatever. Negative training means saying "No" or "Shoo." Do not chase the cat; it will think you are playing. Give it a scratching post to avoid the need for negative training when it comes to clawing.

Some cats will learn to sit up, beg, eat with paws and perform if you reward them with food. But don't expect your cat always to comply. Cats prefer to do tricks when they think it will benefit them, not when you want them to.

CAT MYTH

Cats hate to be walked.

The idea of a cat walking along with a human, or even another cat, goes against all the facts. Adult cats do not pal around together. They do not explore together, hunt together, or do anything else together. It's not in a cat's nature to be led around or to be a pack member.

And yet, there are some cats that like to go for brief walks with their owners. As usual, it all goes back to kittenhood, when at some point the mother cat may have allowed her little ones to tag along on trips away from the nest. When adult cats follow the lead of their owners, they are doing with their present "mother" what they used to do with their real mother.

GROOMING YOUR CAT

MANY CATS NEVER really require grooming help from their owners, but grooming should be a regular part of your relationship. It will give you an opportunity to regularly check your cat's health, and essential grooming will be welcome if the cat ever needs more grooming than it can handle by itself (after it gets into tar or other substances that might be toxic if ingested).

Grooming is best done outside; it keeps the dirt, hair and fleas out of the house, which is nice for everyone, but especially for those who are allergic to cats' fur and skin dust. The next-best places for grooming are the porch, bathroom or utility room. Indoors, stand the cat on paper or plastic.

Inspect the ears, eyes and claws, cleaning ears with cotton wool and olive oil and the eye area with cotton wool and water if necessary. Examine the teeth and, once a week, clean them to prevent tartar build-up. Also examine and trim claws. (See the section, Neutering and Declawing.)

Long-haired cats in the wild moult only in spring, but because domestic cats are kept in artificially lit and heated conditions, they moult all year round. As a result, long-haired cats need daily grooming – two 15–30-minute sessions – otherwise their coats will mat.

Short-haired cats don't need daily grooming because their coats are easier to manage. They also have longer tongues, so they are proficient at self-grooming. Two half-hour sessions a week should be enough.

If grooming is done frequently enough, there should be no signs of matted hair. However, if there are, when grooming take care of those first, with a wide-toothed comb. Various other utensils can be used, including a fine-toothed comb to find fleas and a rubber brush to remove dead hair.

If the coat seems greasy, sprinkle in some talcum powder or dry cleaner from the pet shop, and comb it out quickly. Some owners also use a piece of silk, velvet, or chamois leather to "polish" the coat.

Cats don't usually need bathing, but if your cat's coat is very dirty or greasy, you will need to clean it. Your cat will probably not like water, so give it plenty of love and attention so that the bath session doesn't turn

Above: *Picked up and supported in the right way, most cats will feel quite secure in human arms.*

Left: *Groom short-haired cats with a fine-toothed metal comb (1) working from the head to the tail. A rubber brush (2) won't scratch the skin. Alternatively, use a soft bristle brush (3). Before a show, "polish" the coat with a piece of silk, velvet or chamois leather to bring up the gloss of the coat (4).*

1

2

3

4

into a test of wills. Close all the doors and windows and make sure the bath area is draught-free. Place a rubber mat in the sink, bath, or other basin to keep the cat from slipping. It might also help to let the cat rest its front paws on the rim of the sink.

Fill the sink with two to four inches of warm water and use a sprayer to wet the cat. Water temperature should be as close to the cat's body temperature as possible – 101.4°F. Lather with a nontoxic baby or cat shampoo. Be sure to rinse thoroughly with warm water.

Wrap the cat in a towel before you lift it out and dry it very carefully with a towel or a hair dryer on the low setting. Avoid draughts until the cat is completely dry. Then comb gently through the clean fur.

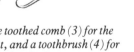

Above: *Grooming equipment should include a slicker brush (1) for long-haired tails, a wire and bristle brush (2), a wide and fine toothed comb (3) for the coat, and a toothbrush (4) for cleaning the face.*

CAT MYTH

Cats always pick the person who hates cats.
Picture yourself entering a roomful of cats much larger and louder than yourself. The cats who like people are staring at you, thinking how beautiful and graceful you are. Their staring makes you feel very uncomfortable. The only cat in the room who is not doing this is the human-hater, who looks away and keeps still, hoping you will ignore it and approach someone else. But, on the contrary, you are in search of a friendly lap on which to sit, and you make a beeline for the anti-human cat, which is not moving, not waving its paws, not meowing, and not staring. This cat is the most nonintimidating one in the room, the one you look to for rescue from these others.

Now, apply that same situation to a cat entering a gathering of humans, and you'll see that its actions are all very "reasoned," given that is doesn't have all the facts. The best recourse for someone who does not like cats is to act like the others who do like cats!

Left: *To groom long-haired cats, use a wide-toothed comb (1) to remove debris and tease out mats. Brush some talcum powder or fuller's earth (2) into the coat to add body. Brush out the powder immediately. Use a wire brush (3) to remove dead hair, paying particular attention to the rump. Gently brush the face area with a toothbrush (4). Run a wide-toothed comb through the hair, upwards towards the back, and fluff out the ruff around the neck (5). For show cats, use a slicker brush on the tail.*

YOUR CAT'S SELF-GROOMING

IT'S EASY TO see how cats acquired their reputation for cleanliness – they spend up to a third of their waking hours grooming themselves. To facilitate this, your cat's barbed tongue can reach almost every part of its body. The forepaws and teeth are also used as cleaning instruments.

Grooming does more than just clean the fur; it also keeps the coat soft and glossy, removes loose and dead hair and skin as well as debris and parasites, tones muscles, and stimulates blood circulation and new growth.

Grooming also has a nutritional function. It provides vitamin D, which is produced on the fur by sunlight. And in hot weather, saliva licked onto the fur performs the same function as sweat, controlling body temperature by evaporation. This explains why cats groom more in warm weather and after periods of play, hunting, or other activity. Cats also groom when they become anxious because it helps them relieve tension.

Mutual grooming is also normal in healthy cats. It carries over from the days when mother groomed the kittens, reinforcing her bond with them and showing them how they could lick each other, especially in hard-to-reach areas like behind the ears.

Although grooming is healthy, some cats practise excessive grooming, causing problems such as skin

Above: Feline mothers are very good teachers, and grooming is one of the first activities kittens learn. The bond between mother and kitten is reinforced during grooming sessions, and appears to give mutual pleasure.

Below: Cats are fastidious about grooming and will spend long, leisurely periods cleaning their coats each day. Using their extremely flexible necks and shoulders, they can reach nearly every part of their body with tongue and teeth.

CAT MYTH

White cats make poor mothers.
Being white does not necessarily make a cat a poor mother. But many white cats are handicapped for motherhood – and for hunting and playing and whatever else they do.

It's not just being white; it's being white with blue eyes. A large majority of such cats are deaf and therefore unaware of noises their kittens are making to tell of their needs.

White cats with orange eyes don't have this handicap. White cats with only one blue eye are deaf only in the ear closest to the blue eye; these cats may be at a disadvantage because they have difficulty telling where a sound is coming from, but generally they make fine mothers.

And even those that are totally deaf are not necessarily inadequate mothers. In fact, many of them compensate for their disability by becoming extra sensitive to vibrations and maximizing their use of visual clues.

Above: *Cats occasionally groom each other – a useful way of getting to those inaccessible places, such as behind the ears.*

Mutual grooming is also a sign of a close bond between cats that share a common territory.

inflammation, hair loss, or development of furballs. Fur is ingested naturally as the cat grooms, but too much grooming causes the mucous in the cat's body to clump the hairs together, resulting in masses that obstruct bowels and interfere with digestive functions. Many cats regurgitate these dark masses of fur automatically (eating grass helps). If yours doesn't, you'll have to purchase a furball cure or give the cat mineral oil to soften the furball and allow it to pass.

At the other extreme, some cats show little interest in grooming. If yours isn't interested, even after contact with dust, dirt or plant burrs, try smearing some butter on its fur. If even that doesn't do it, you'll have to do more than your share of the grooming.

CAT MYTH

Purring always means contentment.
How, where, and why a cat purrs is still something of a mystery. There are even several theories about what part of the cat's body actually produces the sound. But there is no question that purring does not always come from a contented cat.

Most of the time cats purr because of something good. Mother cats purr to show their kittens that they are near. Kittens purr in response to mothers' licking and grooming. Older kittens do it when enticing adults to play. Dominant cats do it when approaching inferior ones in peace or play.

But many are amazed to learn that sick cats, barely able to defend themselves, purr in hopes of soothing a potential aggressor, proving that purring should not be taken as a sign of good health.

NEUTERING AND DECLAWING

NEUTERING AND DECLAWING are two very controversial solutions to two very different feline problems.

Neutering is supported by most experts who work with the world's overpopulation of pets. It is the most effective way to prevent unwanted pregnancies and is done by animal shelters when cats are old enough.

There are several other good reasons to neuter a cat: it makes for a better domestic pet because it prevents spraying and wandering and it actually extends the cat's lifespan by two or three years.

Neutering is best done outside the breeding season, between September and December. It will require an anaesthetic. The best age to castrate males is when they are about five months old, when the blood flow to the testes is relatively light, reducing the risk of pain and post-operative complications. The best age to spay females is when they are about four-and-a-half months old, before they become sexually mature. Owners of pedigreed cats sometimes wait until the cat reaches sexual maturity before neutering to allow full development of all the physical characteristics of the breed.

Opponents of neutering say that a cat still has a right to enjoy sex, and vasectomies and tying of tubes should be performed instead. Some advocate birth control pills or keeping the cats indoors during periods of sexual activity.

Even more controversial than neutering is declawing. Most experts who know cats believe it to be

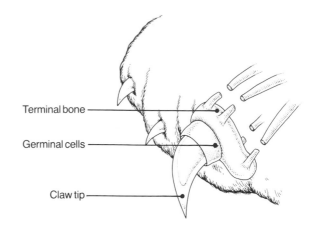

Terminal bone

Germinal cells

Claw tip

Declawing *Under general anaesthetic, the claw is removed, along with the germinal cells responsible for its growth, and part or all of the terminal bone of the toe. This process leaves the animal without its principal means of defence.*

CAT MYTH

Neutered males become fat and lazy.
Several things happen to tom cats that have been neutered. They no longer mate, caterwaul, wander, spray or brawl – all things associated with their sexual maturity. They will be less apt to hunt, kill or climb, or be aggressive to strangers or those in the household – all things not directly associated with their sexual maturity.

But they only become fat and lazy if we do not replace those behaviours with other suitable substitutes. Exercising with a human friend or an animal playmate is necessary. In addition, toms whose energy decreases after neutering should be given about 30 percent less food than they ate before the surgery.

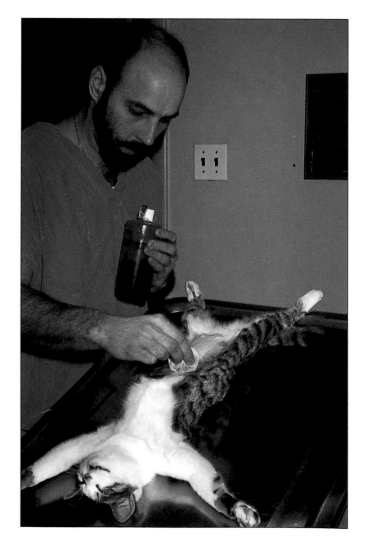

mutilation for the sake of human property. In fact, although the operation is still legal in the United States, it is banned except for medical reasons in Great Britain and many other countries.

Done under general anaesthetic, it removes the claws, the germinal cells and some or all of the terminal bone in the toe. It also happens to remove a cat's main defensive weapons. Declawed cats should not be allowed outdoors because they are totally incapable of climbing or defending themselves.

Ironically, it is the owners who are at fault for cats that constantly scratch. A cat that is properly trained and provided for will not develop the habit of scratching its owner's property. Scratching posts should be provided, and cats should be discouraged with consistent training to avoid scratching anything else.

Claws of healthy, active cats are trimmed down normally with exercise. If your cat is not allowed outdoors, you can trim its claws regularly yourself. Untrimmed claws may grow into the pad of the paw and need veterinary attention.

To trim, hold the cat in your lap and press its paw to make the claws move forward. Before cutting, examine the claw carefully. Cut well clear of the pinkish part that contains nerves. The white tips, however, are dead tissue and should be cut with special clippers made for the purpose. If in doubt, take your cat to a groomer or your vet for trimming.

Above: Eat your heart out, Chris Bonnington! Cats are excellent climbers; using their claws as anchors, they can shin up tree trunks with ease.

Left: Spaying involves removal of the ovaries and uterus in a female cat, preventing breeding. The operation is carried out either through an incision in the flank, or via the abdomen. Spaying of females and neutering of males prevents unwanted kittens and may actually prolong the life of the cat. The cat should be kept indoors for the first few days after the operation.

CAT MYTH

Cats have to sharpen their claws regularly.
Scratching is one of the things humans dislike most about cats. Cats approach an object, usually a treasured piece of furniture, and begin rubbing their claws along it as if to sharpen them.

But it is not necessary for cats to sharpen their claws. The daggerlike protrusions on their paws are being used to mark the territory. Cats possess sweat glands between their paw pads, and the act of scratching serves to secrete a scent, which is transferred to the scratched object. Unless you

can effectively discourage scratching, that cat will consider the scratched area its own, to do with as it likes. In addition, a cat that is not getting enough exercise to wear down its claws naturally may feel the need to "file" them to remove the worn outer covering.

EXERCISE FOR YOUR CAT

UNLIKE HUMANS, CATS don't need 20 minutes of aerobic exercise three times a week to stay in shape. Nor do they need twice-daily walks like canines. But they do need to lead an active life. Outdoor cats will get all the exercise they need by exploring the garden, chasing cats and other intruders, climbing trees, hunting birds, dodging neighbourhood dogs, and just being curious.

Indoor cats who live in flats or houses located in concrete jungles can also be healthy and content, providing they get exercise in other forms. Of course, it also helps to select a breed that is suited to these living conditions, not one known to prefer wandering. Breeds that do not take to total indoor life include Somali, Abyssinian and Rex.

For cats who will give indoor life a shot, scratching posts, climbing frames, tunnel structures and other devices can be used to simulate outdoor activities.

It also helps if you have a companion pet for your cat and if you encourage them to play for an hour or so each day. You can start them off by encouraging them to chase each other around or to run after and swat toys. Soon your cat will keep itself fit and healthy without any effort on your part.

If your cat doesn't object, take it on short walks using a leash. But first you will have to get it used to a collar and leash. Accustom your weaned kitten to wearing a collar with an elastic insertion that acts as a safety device by allowing the cat to escape from the collar if it gets caught on anything. Then attach a long, thin leash or cord to the collar, and start to walk with the cat in the house, then in the garden, then on the pavement. Like anything else you want to persuade your cat to do, it takes patience and regular practice.

Cats will never submit as easily as dogs to being led anywhere. You can never force a cat to walk on a leash if it doesn't want to – unless your cat has a more doglike temperament, as do the Siamese, Burmese, Russian Blue, Colourpoint Shorthairs and Oriental Shorthairs.

Left: Most cats are excellent climbers, delighting in this form of exercise. The climb starts with an agile leap; then the cat propels itself upwards using the strong muscles of the hind limbs and the back. To gain a firm foothold, the claws are extended.

Above right: These kittens are lucky; they have a barn and a large garden in which to work off their surplus energy. For indoor cats, exercise can be encouraged by providing climbing posts, boxes to jump in and out of, and balls to chase.

Below right: While cats are adept at climbing and jumping, getting down again is more of a problem because the claws, which point backwards, do not provide sufficient grip.

Right: *"Cats always land on their feet". This old saying attests to the remarkable agility of the cat, which enables it to fall from considerable heights without injury. When falling, the cat uses its tail to right itself and swivels its body in mid-air so that it is facing the ground, and lands with its back arched to absorb the shock.*

YOUR CAT'S DISORDERS

YOUR CAT MUST be vaccinated against the most widespread and significant viral diseases to which cats are susceptible. Feline distemper, upper respiratory infections and rabies are included in the vaccinations.

Prior to vaccinations, the cat should be eight to twelve weeks old and free of parasites. Plan to deworm the cat approximately two weeks before the immunizations, or have the faeces analyzed to be sure parasites are not present. Remember, when considering contact with pets that may not have been immunized, the vaccination is not effective until about a week after the second dose. Vaccinations also require annual boosters, which can be given when you take your cat to the vet for its annual checkup.

Cats are also susceptible to a variety of other diseases, disorders and parasites, some of which also affect humans. Fleas, ticks, mites. lice and maggots are the major external parasites that you want to check for during regular grooming sessions. Some of these pests transmit diseases and lay eggs on the animal. Check more often if your cat seems to be scratching a lot.

Internal parasites include a variety of worms (round, hook, whip, thread, tape) and single-celled organisms that can wreak havoc where you can't detect it. The protozoa *Toxoplasma gondaii*, found in cat faeces, is particularly significant because it can be transmitted to humans. Pregnant women especially are advised not to handle faeces because the organism can affect the

Below: The observant owner can detect early signs of illness in a cat by monitoring changes in its normal behaviour, and symptoms such as vomiting or coughing. Such clues will help your vet make a quick diagnosis. This chart gives a brief guide to common disorders and their related symptoms.

SYMPTOM / CONDITION	Disorders of the upper respiratory system	Blockage of the intestine	Kidney stones	Distemper	Infectious peritenitis	Wrong diet	Foreign bodies	Fleas	Uterine Infection	Hair balls	Leukaemia	Nephritis	Fungus	Headcold	Shock	Poisoning	Dental problems	Worms	Allergies	Ear Infection
Breathing Difficulties	■								■		■				■	■	■			
Diarrhoea				■							■	■				■	■	■		
Increased thirst				■					■		■	■	■				■			
Vomiting			■	■			■		■	■	■	■	■		■	■	■	■	■	
Fever	■								■		■	■								
Changes in the skin					■								■						■	
Coughing	■								■											
Swollen lymph nodes	■										■				■			■		
Pallor of mucus membranes				■		■					■	■				■	■	■		
Swelling of the body					■			■	■			■								
Constipation			■	■			■		■		■						■	■		
Scratching ears																				■
Shaking head																				■

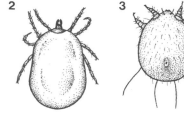

External parasites to watch out for: (1) Lice can cause skin problems. (2) Ticks affect roaming cats and can cause anaemia. (3) Mange mites can cause a highly contagious skin disorder called mange. (4) Fleas, the commonest parasite, can cause dermatitis and even infect the cat with tapeworm.

Left: *Cats are resilient creatures, more resistant to illness than many other animals. Given a well-balanced diet, proper grooming, and lots of tender, loving care, your cat should live a healthy, happy life.*

Below: *During a cat's self-grooming, scratching with the hind legs helps dislodge parasites from the fur.*

unborn child and even cause miscarriage. Regular worming is advised to prevent these problems, which sometimes first manifest themselves as diarrhoea.

Just about every part of a cat's body can be affected by some disease: the skin by ringworm, dermatitis and ulcers; digestion by enteritis, peritonitis, liver and pancreas diseases and obstructions; mouth and teeth by stomatitis; respiratory ailments; eye disorders like conjunctivitis; ear disorders; kidney disease; the circulatory system by anaemia, heartworm and leukaemia.

Be especially wary of your cat's health if it vomits, collapses, has diarrhoea, has trouble breathing, is bleeding, or has dilated pupils. A loss of appetite is probably not serious unless it lasts for more than 24 hours.

During regular grooming sessions and daily contact with your pet, you should check for more subtle signs of disease: listlessness, sneezing, coughing, cloudy eyes, closed eyelids, mouth odour, limping, pain when touched, constipation, frequent urination, and discharges from eyes, ears or nose. Also be wary of any change in regular habits.

Cats begin to show signs of old age after 10 years, which translates to about 60 years in a person's life. (In human terms cats reach age 18 by the end of one year.) The average lifespan for cats is 15 years. Even if they can't live nine lives, they can live a long, healthy one life if given consistent, responsible care.

CAT MYTH

Tom cats regularly and systematically kill kittens.
Far from being regular kitten killers, tom cats have been known to actively participate in the rearing of the young, supposedly to get the queen to detach herself from them and focus back on being in heat for his purposes. Toms have been known to supply food to their broods and to protect the nestful of offspring from intruding humans. Of course, all this observation has taken place in captivity. But that is what the domestic cat is – a captive.

When a tom meets up with its kittens it may care for them; ignore them; it may be driven away by the mother, or, it may kill them. It is thought that the tom kills the kitten accidentally when it is sexually aroused and mounts a female kitten, accidentally killing her with the ritualistic neck bite.

BREEDS OF THE WORLD INTRODUCTION

DIFFERENT BREEDS OF cat have long inhabited many parts of the world. Throughout history migrations of the human population have been accompanied by migrations of the cat population. Since the mid 19th century there has been a great revival of interest in cats and cat breeding on both sides of the Atlantic and many new breeds have come out of North America and Europe. Here the breeds are listed according to country of origin.

On the following pages information is given on the origins of each breed, the physical attributes of the cats, their character, and how to care for them. In the Key Facts boxes, diagrams show how each breed developed.

Naturally occurring

Left: *This symbol is used for a natural population which is now recognized as a breed.*

Cross breeding

Left: *This diagram shows how a man-made breed of cat has been developed by crossing two or more breeds.*

Mutation

Left: *This diagram shows how some breeds of cat come about because a mutation arises within a natural breed. This is due to an unpredictable change occurring in a gene. For example, the blue cat is a mutation of the black.*

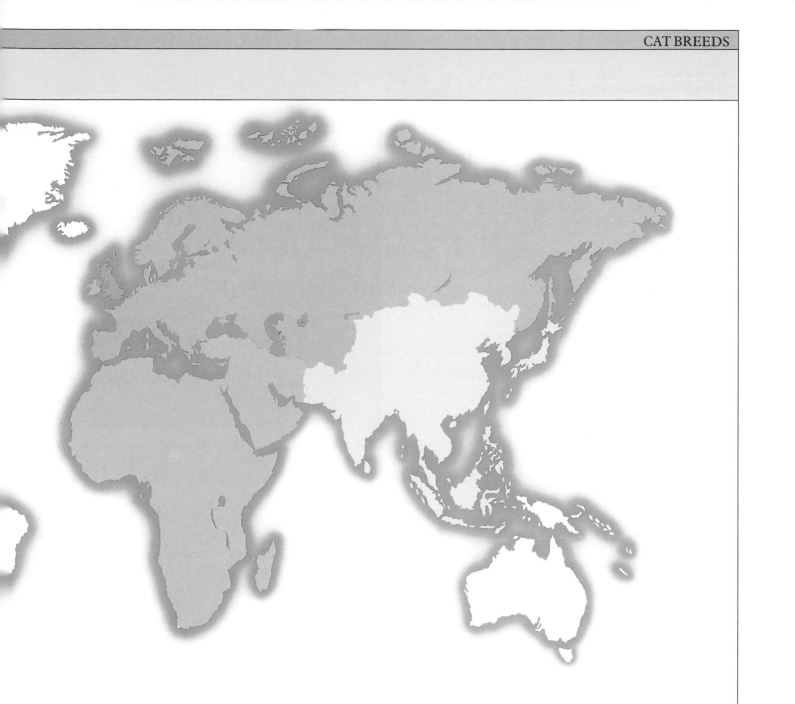

WHITE LONGHAIR (WHITE PERSIAN)

UNTIL THE 16TH CENTURY there were no longhaired cats in Europe. But a few cats of the type now known as Angoras were then introduced from Turkey, along with another, rather heavier longhair from Persia. The modern Persian cat, or Longhair as it is officially known in Britain (although many people still call it Persian and that remains its official name in America), is a descendant of those Persian cats. However, since the types were not always kept separate there was certainly some Angora blood mixed in in the early days of the Cat Fancy.

In Great Britain each colour type of the Longhair is considered an individual breed and, together with other longhaired breeds, they form one of the four groups into which cat breeds can be divided: Longhairs, Siamese, Shorthairs and Foreign Shorthairs. In the United States all the varieties are considered Persians of different colour types.

The White Longhair is a loving cat, quite affection-

Above: *The Orange-Eyed and Copper-Eyed White Longhair are a result of a cross between* *Blue and Cream Longhairs. There is also a White with one blue and one orange eye.*

Varieties: from left to right, Orange-Eyed, Blue-Eyed and Odd-Eyed.

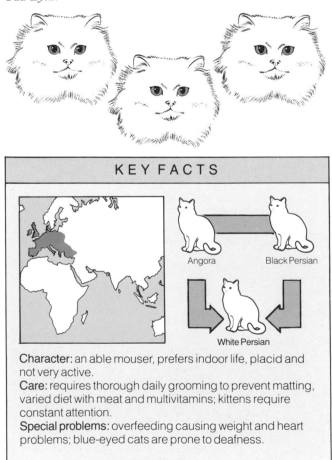

KEY FACTS

Angora   Black Persian

White Persian

Character: an able mouser, prefers indoor life, placid and not very active.
Care: requires thorough daily grooming to prevent matting, varied diet with meat and multivitamins; kittens require constant attention.
Special problems: overfeeding causing weight and heart problems; blue-eyed cats are prone to deafness.

ate towards its owners and those friends of its owners who treat it with respect and kindness. Generally calm, it is more tranquil and less active than many breeds. It is sociable towards other cats and rarely shows its claws. However, this cat can have a temper and can be demanding of affection. A skilled mouser, it also enjoys life inside and is well suited for living in a flat.

There are three varieties of White Longhair: orange-eyed, blue-eyed and odd-eyed. The odd-eyed, with one orange and one blue eye, is the result of interbreeding the other two varieties. Many blue-eyed white cats are born deaf.

The pure white coat of the White Longhair is thick and dense, yet silky. It forms a full frill – a lionlike mane – about the neck and shoulders. The body is of the solid, cobby type, broad but compact and powerful. Short, thick legs end in rounded, large paws. A bushy, short tail ends in a plume. A rounded, broad head features fully developed cheeks and a short nose. The eyes are round and large. The ears are rounded at the tip and relatively small.

Potential pedigree faults include too little hair, too thin a body, a difference in tail colouration, an elongated muzzle and ears that are too close together.

Intensive brushing with a soft-bristle brush is needed daily to prevent matting. The tail is a target for bothersome fleas and should be given particular attention. Dry shampoo should be used regularly.

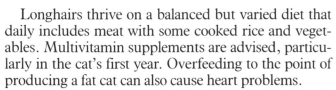

Below: *A White Longhair with blue eyes, displaying the noble beauty for which the breed is famed. The thick, luxuriant fur and the profound expression of the eyes are an irresistible combination. Unfortunately many Blue-Eyed White are born deaf.*

Longhairs thrive on a balanced but varied diet that daily includes meat with some cooked rice and vegetables. Multivitamin supplements are advised, particularly in the cat's first year. Overfeeding to the point of producing a fat cat can also cause heart problems.

During pregnancy and after delivery the female requires a great deal of care, including calcium and vitamin supplements to her normal diet. Likewise young kittens, until the age of four months, need constant attention.

BLACK LONGHAIR (BLACK PERSIAN)

A TRUE BLACK LONGHAIR is a relatively rare animal. Many cats may seem black but on closer inspection actually have white or rust flecks in their coats. The glossy black colour is difficult to breed, and definitive results won't show in kittens until they are six or seven months old. The cat with the true black variation should be discouraged from basking in direct sunlight, which will bleach its coat, and dampness, which will cause a tint of brown. The Black Longhair is lively for a Longhair but retains the characteristic affection for its owners. Its jet black coat is silky and thick with a full frill at the neck and shoulders. The body is the cobby type. It has short, thick legs, rounded, large paws and a short, bushy tail, which ends in a plume. The head is rounded and broad with fully developed cheeks and a short nose. The eyes are round and large, either dark orange or copper in colour. Its ears are rounded at the tip and relatively small.

Common faults are hair not thick enough, a thin body, a tail of a different colour from that of the body, a too-long muzzle, and ears too close together.

To prevent matting, the fur needs daily brushing with a soft-bristle brush, with particular concentration on the tail, where fleas congregate. The diet should include meat, cooked rice and cooked vegetables. Multivitamin supplements are advised, particularly in the cat's first year.

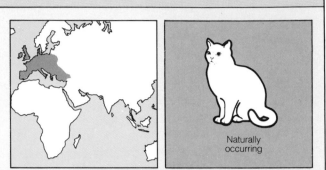

KEY FACTS

Naturally occurring

Character: affectionate and prefers an indoor life, but is lively for a Persian and an able mouser.
Care: requires thorough daily grooming to keep hair free from tangles, varied diet of meat, cooked rice and vegetables, plus multivitamins.
Special problems: true black colouring is difficult to breed.
Pedigree faults: too little hair, thin body, inconsistent tail colourations, ears too close together.

PEKE-FACE PERSIAN

ACTUALLY A VARIETY of the Red Persian – the only variety – the Peke-Face is bred to have a face resembling that of the Pekingese dog: a short nub of a nose, a clear dent between the eyes, wrinkles about the muzzle. This variety is quite rare, as the Red variety from which it springs is very rare itself.

The Peke-Face occurs naturally as a mutation of the Red or Red Tabby Persian, and it is encouraged in the United States. However, it is not encouraged in Great Britain because its compressed face is basically a deformity that can cause breathing, tear duct and eating problems.

Apart from the face, the Peke-Face carries most of the Persian traits. The ears are rounded, small and tufted. Its fur is thick and silky, and of the Red or Red Tabby colouring. The body is of the solid, cobby type, with short, thick legs and round, large paws. The tail is short and bushy, ending in a plume.

Generally a calm cat, the Peke-Face Persian is affectionate towards its owners and others whom it has come to know as kind and gentle. It rarely shows its claws and gets along well with other cats, although it can have a bit of a temper. Life indoors is just fine for this cat. As with all Persians, the fur must be brushed daily with a soft-bristle brush to prevent matting.

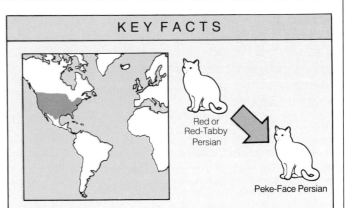

KEY FACTS

Red or Red-Tabby Persian → Peke-Face Persian

Character: calm, affectionate, sociable, prefers an indoor life.
Care: requires thorough daily grooming to prevent matting.
Special problems: possible respiratory and eating difficulties and overcrowding of the teeth, due to compression of facial features. Running eyes due to distortion of eye ducts.

CAMEO LONGHAIR (CAMEO PERSIAN)

A RELATIVE NEWCOMER, the Cameo Longhair was developed in the 1950s by crossbreeding Smoke and Tortoiseshell Persians. It has a white undercoat that is tipped with cream, red, tortoiseshell, or tabby in one of three ways:

Shell Cameo's fur has very short colour tipping on the end of each hair that give the coat a cloudy appearance. Shaded Cameos have tipping which extends further down each hair which renders a dazzling sheen to the coat. And Smoke Cameos have very long tips that hide the white undercoat until the cat is in motion.

The colours and tip types combine to produce eight recognized varieties of the Cameo Longhair. Cream Shell Cameo has short cream tips. Red Shell Cameo has short red tips. Cream Shaded Cameo has medium cream tips. Red Shaded Cameo has medium red tips. Cream Smoke Cameo has long cream tips. Red Smoke Cameo has long red tips. Cameo Tabby has cream and red tips of any length. Cameo Tortoiseshell has red, cream and black tips of any length. In all eight varieties the eyes should be copper.

Cameo Longhairs are affectionate cats, like most Longhairs. They are quick to recognize who will treat them gently and with kindness and will respond most lovingly to those individuals. Other cats are generally welcome in the home, and the Cameo Longhair usually keeps its claws retracted. Skilled mousers, they enjoy some outdoor time, but they are equally happy in a small flat.

Their coats have not lost the thick, dense, silky feel of the classic Persian, complete with the full frill about

Above: *This Lilac-Tortie kitten displays the classic "Persian" features: broad face, large, round eyes, ears with handsome interior tufts, stocky body and luxuriant coat.*

*Left: Shaded Cameos possess a creamy white undercolour overlaid with cream to red tipping, which is deepest around the head, along the back and on the legs and feet. Kittens are virtually white at birth, only later developing their characteristic colouring. Both the Cream Shaded **left** and the Red Shaded **right** have eyes of a deep orange or copper, with a pleasing expression.*

Varieties: from left to right, Cream Shell Cameo, Red Shell Cameo, Cream Shaded Cameo, Red Smoke Cameo, Tabby and Cameo Tortoiseshell.

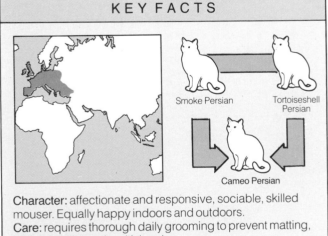

KEY FACTS

Smoke Persian   Tortoiseshell Persian

Cameo Persian

Character: affectionate and responsive, sociable, skilled mouser. Equally happy indoors and outdoors.
Care: requires thorough daily grooming to prevent matting, balanced diet and multivitamins.
Special problems: overfeeding causing weight and heart problems. Tail can be a target for fleas.
Pedigree faults: too little hair, thin body, inconsistent tail colour, elongated muzzle, ears too close together.

the neck and shoulders. A solid, stocky body and short, thick legs form the typical Persian frame. Large, round paws and a bushy, short tail, ending in a plume, complete the picture.

The head is round and broad, with fully developed cheeks and a short nose. The eyes are round and large. The ears are rounded at the tip, relatively small, and tufted.

Potential pedigree faults include too little hair, too thin a body, a difference in tail colouration, an elongated muzzle, and ears that are too close together.

Intensive brushing with a soft-bristle brush is needed daily to prevent matting in the fur. The tail, a target for fleas, needs particular attention. Dry shampoo should be used regularly. Meat with cooked rice and vegetables are the basis for a balanced diet but should be supplemented with a multivitamin, particularly in the cat's first 12 months. Like most Longhairs, the Cameos will overeat if allowed to do so.

SMOKE LONGHAIR (SMOKE PERSIAN)

THIS CAT FIRST appeared at shows in Great Britain in the 1870s, the result of crossbreeding of Black, Blue and Chinchilla Persians. Although the coat appears to be of one solid colour, the effect is actually achieved by very long and very dark tipping. The pale undercoat is revealed only as the cat moves.

There are three varieties: Black Smoke Longhair, Blue Smoke Longhair, and Smoke Tortoiseshell Longhair (which is red, cream and black). Each variety has orange eyes.

The fur is silky, thick, and dense, with a full frill that is white. The cobby-type body is stocky and broad, with short, thick legs and large, round paws. The short, bushy tail ends in a plume. The head is round and broad, the cheeks are full and the nose is short. The eyes are round and large. The ears are rounded, small, and tufted.

This cat is a good mouser but enjoys its home life as well. It demonstrates its affection for the family and friends and expects affection in return. Generally even-tempered, the Smoke Longhair accepts other cats into the household.

As with all Longhairs, the fur must be brushed daily with a soft-bristle brush to prevent matting of the fur.

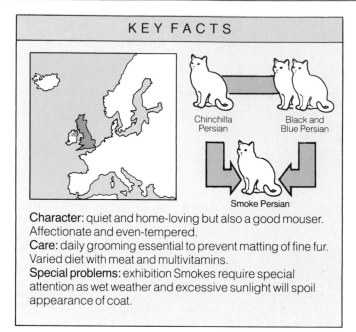

KEY FACTS

Chinchilla Persian

Black and Blue Persian

Smoke Persian

Character: quiet and home-loving but also a good mouser. Affectionate and even-tempered.
Care: daily grooming essential to prevent matting of fine fur. Varied diet with meat and multivitamins.
Special problems: exhibition Smokes require special attention as wet weather and excessive sunlight will spoil appearance of coat.

Meat is a favoured diet item, balanced with cooked rice and vegetables. Multivitamin supplements are recommended, particularly during pregnancy and for kittens and growing cats.

Right: The Smoke Longhair is a magnificent breed, and still relatively rare. This Black Smoke displays the characteristic silvery ruff around the neck, contrasting with the black head and striking orange eyes. The smoke's coat is long, dense and silky, with a very long frill, and requires even more frequent grooming that that of some other Longhairs.

Left: The Blue Smoke resembles the Blue Longhair, but when it moves the contrasting white of the undercoat becomes visible. The Blue Smoke is difficult to breed without tabby markings.

Varieties: from left to right, Black Smoke, Blue Smoke and Smoke Tortoiseshell.

CHINCHILLA LONGHAIR

KEY FACTS

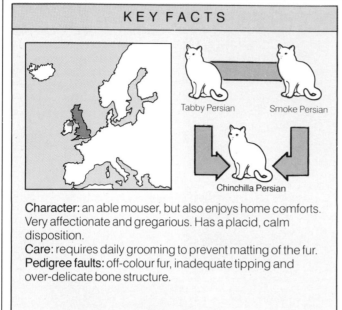

Tabby Persian　　Smoke Persian

Chinchilla Persian

Character: an able mouser, but also enjoys home comforts. Very affectionate and gregarious. Has a placid, calm disposition.
Care: requires daily grooming to prevent matting of the fur.
Pedigree faults: off-colour fur, inadequate tipping and over-delicate bone structure.

THIS CAT IS named for the chinchilla, a South American rodent sought after for its intensely soft fur. The Chinchilla Longhair sports a similarly soft and sparklingly white coat, but, while the chinchilla has a darker undercoat tipped with white, the fur of its namesake cat is white tipped with black. The tipping occurs most noticeably in the face, at the ears and along the back.

When the tipping extends a little further down each hair, producing a silver-grey effect over a white

Varieties: Shaded Silver.

undercoat, the variety is known as the Shaded Silver.

The thin bone structure and finely tipped fur give the Chinchilla Longhair the appearance of quite a delicate creature, but it is nevertheless generally a healthy and robust cat.

The breed is a "manmade" Longhair, having first appeared in various cross-breedings of Persians in the early 1900s and then being selectively bred to enhance the special characteristics.

Like most Persians, it is an able mouser, although perfectly suited for a totally indoor existence. It forms strong attachments to people who show it some affection and it can become fairly demanding of frequent attention. The Chinchilla Longhair has a generally calm disposition, and is quite sociable to-

wards other cats. It is content to spend a great deal of its time at rest.

The fur is thick and dense, but quite silky. It gives the entire head and body a singular round appearance. The body is cobby, like most Persians, but with a slightly thinner bone structure. The legs are short and thick with rounded, large paws and the tail is short and bushy. The rounded, broad head has full cheeks and chin, and a short nose. The eyes are large and rounded: green or blue-green in the white Chinchilla Longhair and green in the shaded silver variety. The ears are

Above: *One of the most beautiful of the long-haired breeds, the Chinchilla Longhair has become a symbol of luxury, even decadence. Appearances are deceptive: these delicate-looking creatures are in fact quite tough and will hunt mice along with the best of them.*

rounded at the tip and small.

Daily brushing with a very soft bristle brush is needed to prevent matting of the fur.

Standard faults are off-colour fur, inadequate tipping and too delicate a bone structure.

BICOLOUR LONGHAIR

Varieties: top from left to right, Cream and Chocolate: bottom from left to right: Red, Black and Blue.

KEY FACTS

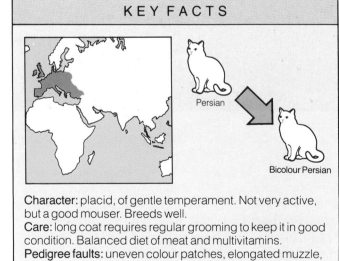

Persian

Bicolour Persian

Character: placid, of gentle temperament. Not very active, but a good mouser. Breeds well.
Care: long coat requires regular grooming to keep it in good condition. Balanced diet of meat and multivitamins.
Pedigree faults: uneven colour patches, elongated muzzle, ears too close together, hair or body too thin.

WHEN THESE CATS first appeared at shows, they were placed in the "any other colour" class. But eventually, as they demonstrated their staying power, they were given a class of their own. The original standards mandated an exact symmetry in their patching, but today any even patching is acceptable.

A beautifully contrasting cat, the Bicolour Longhair features solid colours with white muzzle, chest, undersides, legs and feet. A white frill also is now permitted. Any recognized solid colour with white is an acceptable Bicolour Longhair variety. The eye colour should complement the solid colour.

It's an affectionate cat, good-natured towards other creatures that treat it kindly and gently. Not an overly energetic cat, it is nonetheless a good mouser. It's perfectly content with life in a flat, although periods outside are appreciated.

In typical Longhair fashion, the coat is thick and dense, yet silky with the lionlike frill about the neck and shoulders. The body is solid, broad and powerful. The short, thick legs have rounded, large paws. A bushy, short tail ends in a plume. The rounded, broad head features fully developed cheeks, a short nose, round and large eyes, and relatively small ears that are rounded at the tip and tufted.

Potential pedigree faults include uneven colour patches, too little hair, too thin a body, a difference in tail colouration, an elongated muzzle and ears that are too close together.

Intensive brushing with a soft-bristle brush is needed daily to prevent matting of the fur.

Left and above: The Bicolour Longhair has a coat comprised of a solid colour broken by white. The main Bicolour varieties are Black-and-White, Blue-and-White, Cream-and-White and Red-and-White. For show purposes the patches of colour must be clearly delineated; not more than half the coat should be white, and up to two-thirds can be coloured. The face should be patched with colour and white.

TORTOISESHELL LONGHAIR

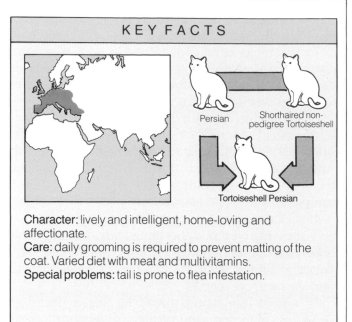

KEY FACTS

Persian

Shorthaired non-pedigree Tortoiseshell

Tortoiseshell Persian

Character: lively and intelligent, home-loving and affectionate.
Care: daily grooming is required to prevent matting of the coat. Varied diet with meat and multivitamins.
Special problems: tail is prone to flea infestation.

THIS VERY RARE Persian is difficult to breed and consequently carries a higher price tag than most of the others. The genetic make-up necessary to produce the Tortoiseshell Persian also guarantees that the resulting cat is always female.

The cat was produced through the accidental crossing of Persians with nonpedigree, and probably shorthaired, tortoiseshell cats. Those individuals with a red or cream facial blaze from nose to forehead are much sought after.

Apart from its wild-looking coat, the Tortoiseshell Longhair is a typical "Persian". Affectionate and good-natured towards most other creatures that treat it kindly and gently, the cat forms attachments to the family as well as frequent-visiting friends. Life indoors is acceptable to this calm cat that enjoys the comforts of home.

The coat is silky, thick and dense. The customary Persian frill about the neck and shoulders might appear a bit "wilder" in this cat than in other Longhairs. The body is solid, broad and powerful. Short, thick legs end in rounded, large paws. A bushy, short tail ends in a plume.

The rounded, broad head can have a false heart-shape appearance in those individual cats with facial blazes. Otherwise, the features are full cheeks, a short nose, round and large eyes and relatively small ears that are rounded at the tip and tufted.

Intensive brushing with a soft-bristle bush is needed daily to prevent matting of the fur. Particular attention must be paid to the tail, where fleas can gather.

TORTOISESHELL-AND-WHITE LONGHAIR

THE TORTOISESHELL-AND-WHITE Longhair has the three tortoiseshell colours: black, red and cream (or their dilute forms with chocolate, blue or lilac replacing black), well distributed and broken and interspersed with white. In America some bodies recognize

a similar cat but most call it the Calico Persian – because of a resemblance of the fur to a popular cotton print – and describe it as a white cat with black and red patching, much more white being apparent than in the British type and the underparts especially being white. Like the Tortoiseshell, this is a sex-linked variety and it appears in females only.

It's a loving cat, quite affectionate towards its owners and those friends of its owners who treat it with respect and kindness. Generally calm, the Tortoiseshell and White is more tranquil and less active than many breeds. It is sociable towards other cats and rarely shows its claws. However, this cat can have a temper and can be demanding of affection. A skilled mouser, it also enjoys life inside.

The fur is silky, thick and dense. It forms a full frill about the neck and shoulders. The body is of the solid, cobby type, broad, compact and powerful.

Intensive brushing with a soft-bristle brush is needed daily.

KEY FACTS

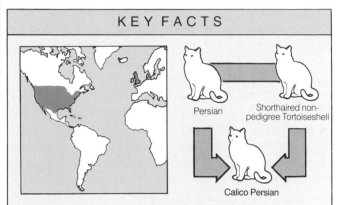

Persian

Shorthaired non-pedigree Tortoiseshell

Calico Persian

Character: has a placid, gentle temperament, not very active. Sociable and very affectionate, but demanding. A skilled mouser, well suited to indoor and outdoor life.
Care: requires thorough daily grooming to prevent matting of the fur. Varied diet with meat and multivitamins.

COLOURPOINT LONGHAIR (HIMALAYAN)

OFTEN MISTAKEN FOR a long-haired Siamese because its colour patterns are similar, the Himalayan is nonetheless of Longhair Persian type and in Britain is considered a variation of Longhair/Persian. It's the product of a purposeful crossbreeding of Siamese, Birman and Persian that first bore fruit in the mid-1930s. It has the stocky, solid body and the dense, silky coat of the Persian, but the point-markings of the Siamese. Its American name is borrowed from the Himalayan rabbit of the same colouration.

Debutante, who was the first of the pointed Long-

Below: A Seal-Tabby-Point. The body should be a light creamy colour and the mask *clearly marked, especially around the eyes and nose.*

hairs, was born in 1935 at the Harvard Medical School. Pedigree breeding began in 1950, but most cautious breeders waited until 1957 before showing the cats in San Diego, California.

There are seven varieties recognized as Himalayan in the United States: Blue-Point, with grey-blue points (tail, feet, legs, ears, mask); Chocolate-Point, with milk-chocolate brown points; Seal-Point, with seal-brown points; Flame-Point, with orange-red points; Lilac-Point, with pink-grey points; Blue-Cream-Point, with creamy blue or white points; and Tortoiseshell-Point, with cream and red patching on the points. Other varieties appear in Britain and all have the sapphire-blue eyes of their Siamese ancestors.

At birth the distinctive point markings are barely visible on the white kitten. They are established at six months but take the first 18 months of the cat's life to reach their full mature shading.

The Himalayan is a cat filled with character, at once inquisitive and enterprising but also exceptionally devoted to its owner. It often manifests doglike traits in learning and obedience and tags along about the house with the owner. Playful but gentle, it is quite forgiving of slights against itself. This cat is a good mouser and enjoys a bit of open space occasionally, but it is well adapted for an indoor existence.

The Persian characteristics are dominant in most physical aspects of the Himalayan, apart from its colouring. The fur is silky, thick and dense, with an abundant ruff. A solid, cobby-type body stands squarely on short, thick legs, ending in round and large paws. The head is round and broad, with fully developed cheeks, a short nose and large, round eyes. It rests on a short, thick neck. The tail is short and bushy, ending in a plume. The ears are small, rounded and tufted.

Regular brushing with a soft-bristle brush is needed to maintain the Persian coat and to prevent matting.

Standard faults are poor bone structure, crossed eyes, nonblue eyes, short hair, a triangular shape to the head and nonstandard markings.

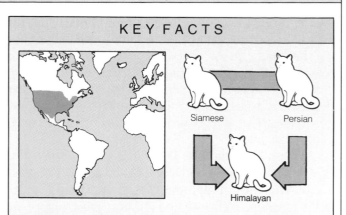

KEY FACTS

Siamese   Persian

Himalayan

Character: intelligent and playful, gentle, very affectionate and devoted. Seeks a lot of attention. A skilled mouser, but also well suited to indoor life.
Care: requires regular grooming to keep the hair free from tangles. Varied diet with meat, cooked rice and vegetables.
Pedigree faults: crossed eyes, poor bone structure, non-blue eyes, non-standard markings.

Left: The Colourpoint Longhair, of which this Chocolate-Point is a striking example, combines the point markings of the Siamese with the body type and coat length of the Longhair Persian. Show judges look for deep points and a pale body colour; the long coat causes lighter coloration in the points than that found in the Siamese, but it makes the pale body colour easier to achieve.

Varieties: from left to right, Blue-Point, Chocolate-Point, Seal-Point, Flame-Point, Lilac-Point and Tortoiseshell-Point.

LILAC LONGHAIR (LAVENDER KASHMIR)

AN OFFSHOOT OF selective breeding for Himalayans, the lilac colour of this cat's coat is a dilution which is linked to the Siamese so, although accepted as a colour variation of the Longhair in Britain, in the United States it is seen as a separate breed called Lavender Kashmir. It has the copper or orange eyes and the thick, silky coat of its Persian ancestors but with a new, pink-grey tint.

As with Persians, the body is a solid, cobby type with short, thick legs and large, round paws. The tail is bushy and ends in a plume. The round head features fully developed cheeks and a short nose. Eyes are round and large. Ears are relatively small, rounded at their tips, and well tufted.

KEY FACTS

Siamese   Persian

Kashmir

Character: curious and enterprising, likes to be active. Very affectionate and loyal.
Care: thorough and regular grooming required to keep the coat in good condition. Needs a varied diet with meat, cooked rice and vegetables.

Because of its Persian-type coat, the Lavender Kashmir requires daily brushing with a soft-bristle brush to prevent matting. It's a good mouser and enjoys some time outdoors, but it is equally happy with an indoor existence.

CHOCOLATE-TORTOISESHELL LONGHAIR

KEY FACTS

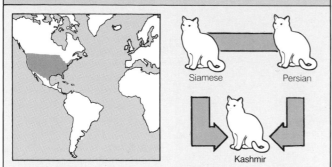

Siamese   Persian

Kashmir

Character: curious and enterprising, likes to be active. Very affectionate and loyal.
Care: thorough and regular grooming required to keep the coat in good condition. Needs a varied diet with meat, cooked rice and vegetables.

ANOTHER BYPRODUCT OF selective breeding for Himalayans, the Chocolate-Tortoiseshell Longhair Kashmir has only recently been admitted to show status.

An affectionate cat with a great curiosity about everything around it, the Chocolate-Tortoiseshell Kashmir is most content when doing something. It generally becomes deeply devoted to its owner. It is more active than most of its Longhair Persian ancestors.

The fur has the density, thickness and silky feel of a Longhair and is in patches of red, cream and chocolate-brown. The body is solid and stocky, and the legs are short and thick, ending in large, round paws. The tail is bushy and ends in a plume. The round head features fully developed cheeks and a short nose. Eyes are round and large and are copper or orange in colour.

Ears are relatively small, rounded at their tips, and heavily tufted.

The coat of the Chocolate-Tortoiseshell Longhair Kashmir requires daily brushing with a soft-bristle brush to prevent matting. It's a good mouser and enjoys some time outdoors, but it is equally happy with an indoor existence.

Some other offshoots of the Himalayan breeding programmes that also now have show standards are the Chinchilla Golden Longhair Persian, which has light brown tips on a cream coat and green eyes; the Shaded Golden Longhair Persian, which has deeper brown tips on a cream coat and green eyes; the Lilac-Cream Longhair Kashmir, which has a pink-grey and cream coat and copper-coloured eyes; and the Chestnut-Brown Longhair Kashmir, which has a coat that ranges from medium to dark brown and has copper-coloured eyes.

BIRMAN

Left: The Birman is also known as the Sacred Cat of Burma, but it is not related to the Burmese. There are several varieties of Birman, all of which share the characteristic feature of pure white "gloves" on all four paws. On the hind paws the white gloves extend up the back of the hocks to end in points known as "laces". The eyes are bright china blue and of enigmatic expression. As this Blue-Point shows, the Birman's coat is shorter and silkier than that of the Persian, and the body is slimmer.

THE EXACT ANCESTRY of the Birman is not known, but it is speculated that the first of the line lived in Buddhist temples in Burma, under the protection of the Grand Lama. They were revered as near-deities.

Legend offers a much more interesting version of the Birman's beginnings. According to the folk tale, the cats lived with the holy men in the temples. During an invasion by foreign armies, the cat of the High Priest discovered its dying master at the foot of a golden statue of a goddess that had sapphires for its eyes. The cat leaped onto the statue and, as it landed there, the soul of the High Priest was transported from man into cat. Instantly the white colouring of the cat was replaced by gold, and its yellow eyes changed to the colour of the precious stones in the eyes of the statue. Its points (muzzle, ears, legs, feet and tail) transformed to a dark colouring, except where they had touched their master – the feet retained their original white colour. This miracle had such a powerful impact on the priests that they drove off the invading armies. From that point forward, all temple cats had the Birman colouring.

Today's Birman has a white or pale-tinted coat with darker points, white-tipped front paws, and white-gloved rear paws with a bit of white running up the back of the legs. There are four widely accepted varieties: Seal-Point Birman (closest to the legendary cat), with a pale golden coat and brown points; Lilac-Point Birman, with an off-white body and pink-grey points; Blue-Point Birman, with a blue-white coat and blue-grey points; and Chocolate-Point Birman, with a yellow-white coat and milk-chocolate points.

KEY FACTS

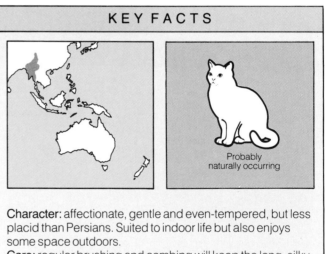

Probably naturally occurring

Character: affectionate, gentle and even-tempered, but less placid than Persians. Suited to indoor life but also enjoys some space outdoors.
Care: regular brushing and combing will keep the long, silky coat in good condition. Prefers a diet of pure meat.
Pedigree faults: crossed or off-colour eyes, pointed muzzle, deformed tail.

Varieties: from left to right, Seal-Point, Lilac-Point, Blue-Point and Chocolate Point.

The Birman has a longer body and narrower face than most other long-haired breeds. The legs are medium in length, with large and round paws. Its fur is silky, longer on the neck and tail, feathered on the tail, and often wavy on the underside. The head is round with fully developed cheeks, a medium size nose, and heavy whiskers. The round eyes have a slight slant to them. Ears are round tipped and medium in size.

Standard faults include crossed or off-colour eyes, a pointed muzzle and deformed tail.

The Birman is a sociable, gentle cat that shows affection most to those humans who share its tranquil characteristics. However, it will become quite devoted to the entire family. It is comfortable indoors and very well behaved living in a flat, but it enjoys time outdoors in familiar surroundings when the weather is pleasant. It practises much self-control over its appetite and prefers pure meat. Regular brushing and combing is suggested for the coat, although it does not have a tendency to mat.

Females are very open to mating, with great frequency, and must be closely monitored because of this. Kittens are born with solid colouring, obtaining their darker points in four or five months.

Above: *A Seal-Point Birman, one of only four colours (along with Blue-Point, Chocolate and Lilac) which are widely recognised.*

BALINESE

A LONG-HAIRED SIAMESE, the Balinese first appeared as a long-haired mutation in a litter of Siamese kittens in the United States in the 1950s. When breeders challenged the cat as not fitting standards for the breed, it was designated the Balinese. There is no connection with Bali beyond the name and the similarity of the cat's graceful movements to those of the dancers of the island. The breed was first recognized in the United States in 1968, and did not receive full championship status in Britain until 1986.

The new breed inherited the slender, lithe body, the wedge-shaped head, and the sapphire-blue eyes of the Siamese, but with a longer coat. By comparison to other longhairs, such as the Persian, the coat of the Balinese is relatively short.

Its manners are also those of the Siamese, craving attention and play, enjoying the company of humans,

Varieties: from left to right, Seal-Point, Blue-Point and Chocolate-Point and Lilac-Point.

affectionate towards the family, but devoted primarily to one person. Some individual cats can also exhibit the aloofness of the Siamese. The Balinese is an appropriate cat for life in a flat, but it does enjoy the open spaces of a terrace or garden. Its movements are graceful, almost acrobatic.

Varieties are the same as those in the Siamese breed: Seal-Point Balinese, with cream coat with seal-brown points; Blue-Point Balinese, with blue-white coat with blue-grey points; Chocolate-Point Balinese, with yellow-white coat with chocolate-brown points; Lilac-Point Balinese, white coat with pink-grey points. In Britain Red-Point, Cream-Point and all the tortoiseshell and tabby variations are also recognized.

The fur is medium long without an undercoat or the

ruff characteristic of many long-haired cats. The head is wedge shaped, with a long nose, pointed and large ears, medium-sized eyes that are almond shaped and slanted. The long body shows good muscling and ends in a medium fluffy tail. Legs are long but the forelegs are shorter than the hind legs. The paws are egg shaped and small.

The Balinese is not finicky in its diet. Its fur should be brushed and combed daily, although it is not nearly as likely to mat as that of the Persian.

Litters of three or four kittens are born to attentive parents that spend a great deal of time in play with their offspring. The Balinese reaches sexual maturity much earlier than other long-haired cats.

Below: The Balinese is essentially a long-haired Siamese and possesses the same characteristic point markings.

The coat is long and silky and the long tail has a plumed appearance. This one is a Tortoiseshell-Point.

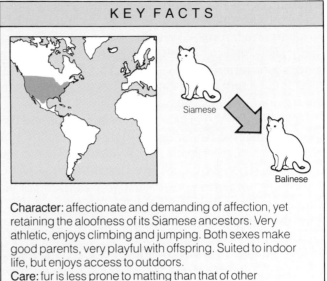

KEY FACTS

Siamese

Balinese

Character: affectionate and demanding of affection, yet retaining the aloofness of its Siamese ancestors. Very athletic, enjoys climbing and jumping. Both sexes make good parents, very playful with offspring. Suited to indoor life, but enjoys access to outdoors.
Care: fur is less prone to matting than that of other long-haired breeds, but daily grooming is appreciated.

ANGORA (TURKISH ANGORA)

ANGORA CATS WERE the first long-haired breeds introduced into Europe; this was in the 16th century. They were imported from a city of the same name in Turkey (now called Ankara), the city that produced the Angora goat, characterized by its extremely soft hair that is commonly referred to as mohair. The cats quickly won the attention of cat enthusiasts.

However, as the Persian breed began to capture the spotlight, the true Angora came close to extinction as a breed. Interest grew again after World War II, and the breed was revived by U.S. breeders under the name Turkish Angora using existing cats and some imported directly from the Ankara Zoo.

In the United States today, several varieties of the Turkish Angora are recognized.

The Angora is a well-mannered, affectionate and intelligent cat. It seems to enjoy life most with a single person who shares its respect for peace and quiet. Playful at times, it is nonetheless strictly a cat for indoors, so long as that environment is not too tightly confined.

The varieties include: White Angora, with traditional colour and orange, blue, or odd eyes; Black Angora, with orange eyes; Blue Angora, with orange eyes; Black Smoke Angora, with white coat with black tips and orange eyes; Blue Smoke Angora, with white coat with blue tips and orange eyes; Blue Tabby Angora, with blue-white coat with blue marking and orange eyes; Silver Tabby Angora, with silver coat with black marking and green or hazel eyes; Red Tabby Angora, with red coat with darker red marking

and orange eyes; Brown Tabby Angora, with brown coat with black marking and orange eyes; Calico Angora, with white coat with black and red patches and orange eyes; Bicolour Angora, with white coat with cream, red, blue or black marking and orange eyes. The full colour range is not yet established in Britain but could also include Caramel and Cinnamon and Tipped and Tortoiseshell varieties. Kittens, which are active and playful at a very early age, do not develop the true Angora coat until after the age of two years.

The fur is silky, fine textured, and medium in

Left: *The Angora is an elegant cat, its slender body dressed in fine, silky plumes. The head is long and tapers towards the chin, and the ears are large and pointed, with interior tufts. Although bred in other colours, the Odd-Eyed White (Ankara Kedi) is accepted as the natural form of the breed. Shown here are a Cinammon and a Blue Tabby.*

Varieties: from left to right, Brown Tabby, White with blue eyes, Calico, Blue with orange eyes, Black Smoke with orange eyes, Silver Tabby.

KEY FACTS

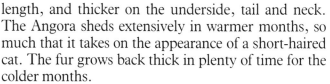

Naturally occurring

Character: a one-person cat, gentle and quiet, but playful. Prefers indoor life, but needs adequate space for exercise.
Care: daily brushing and combing, especially in the warmer months, when it moults heavily.
Special problems: blue-eyed cats are often born deaf.

length, and thicker on the underside, tail and neck. The Angora sheds extensively in warmer months, so much that it takes on the appearance of a short-haired cat. The fur grows back thick in plenty of time for the colder months.

The head is long and wedge shaped with a long nose; the eyes are medium sized, almond shaped and slanted, and the ears are pointed, large and tufted. The body is long and slender, with fragile bone structure. The legs are long and thin, with the forelegs a bit shorter than the hind legs. The long tail is tapered but ends in a plume.

The Angora's coat should be brushed and combed daily. It is much easier to brush than that of the Longhair because it lacks an undercoat. It is not a finicky eater but prefers meat.

Standard faults are spotting on the body, a short tail, and short or wavy hair. Blue-eyed individuals are often born deaf.

MAINE COON

Left: The Brown Tabby-and-White form of Maine Coon remains the most popular.

ONE DAY A domestic cat and a wild raccoon achieved the genetic impossibility of a successful mating. Their offspring were the very first Maine Coon cats, or so the lore of this breed would have us believe.

Actually, this distinctive American breed developed from American farm cat stock, which itself was the result of crossings of nonpedigree short-hairs and Angoras brought back to Maine by sailors. The Maine Coon was quite popular at U.S. shows in the 19th century, but interest declined with the introduction of Persians. It remained a welcome house pet, and in the 1950s exhibit interest began to resurface.

It is an excellent family cat, with its large, sturdy build, healthy constitution and intelligence.

More than any other long-haired breed, the Maine Coon needs lots of open space. It enjoys the comforts of home, but it must have access to a garden and particularly likes a good, active romp in the outdoors. It needs to practise its mousing skills. Possibly because of its rough, outdoor, fend-for-yourself ancestry that led the breed to become accustomed to make-do sleeping arrangements, the Maine Coon will often be found asleep in unusual positions.

Practically any of the standard colours and patterns are acceptable in this breed, with the exception of Chocolate-Point, Lilac-Point and Siamese. Copper, gold and green eyes are permitted in all varieties, with blue and odd-eyed also acceptable in the White Maine Coon.

The fur is extremely thick and shaggy, shorter near the head and front shoulders. The body is noticeably large, with a great deal of muscular definition. The tail is long and bushy, ending in a small plume. The legs are medium in length and very muscular, ending in round, large paws. The head is large and round, with a medium nose. It has large eyes, and ears that are large, pointed, thickly tufted, and carried erect.

Daily brushing with a soft-bristle brush is advised to prevent matting of the thick, heavy coat. The Maine Coon's diet should alternate between meat and fish. It is one of the healthiest cat breeds, able to endure wide ranges in temperature for prolonged periods – a hearkening back to its hardy ancestry.

A litter holds two or three kittens, which very likely will bear little resemblance to one another. They develop slowly and won't reach full maturity until the age of four years.

The Maine Coon is very rare in Europe, where a similar breed – the Norwegian Forest Cat – has evolved. Standard faults in the Maine Coon are poor muscling and a thin coat.

Angora

Non-pedigree shorthair

Maine Coon

Character: amiable and amusing, an ideal domestic pet. Enjoys indoor life, but must have access to open space outdoors. An able mouser, tough, rugged and agile.
Care: thick, heavy coat requires thorough daily grooming. Varied diet of meat and fish.
Pedigree faults: poor muscling and thin coat.

Right: *A Silver Tabby Maine Coon, showing off its smooth, shaggy coat and bushy tail. The large, tapering ears have horizontal tufts, and the eyes are round and expressive.*

Varieties: *from left to right, Silver Tabby, Black Smoke, Calico, Blue and White Bicolour, Brown Tabby and Red Mackerel.*

89

SOMALI

THE SOMALI IS a medium to long-haired mutation of the Abyssinian, the result of long-haired genes introduced into the Abyssinian in Great Britain in the early 1900s. It was first bred in the United States in the 1960s. The result was a cat with a "wild" appearance but with the graceful body structure of the Oriental breeds.

It is a very intelligent cat that eagerly learns tricks quickly. However, it does love the feeling of freedom and will grow quite restless when kept closely confined indoors. This is not a good indoor cat.

The Somali also takes its time in coming to show affection for its owners. It needs to be certain of mutual trust and respect and can itself be mistrustful at times. Some individuals of this breed can also display excessive shyness.

There are three varieties: Sorrel or Red Somali, red-brown ticked with bands of chocolate-brown; usual or Ruddy Somali, brown ticked with bands of darker brown or black; and Blue Somali, blue-grey ticked with bands of the darker version of the same. Some breeders are introducing other varieties.

The fur is medium long and just a bit shaggy. The body is long and slender, with a back that is slightly arched and a long tail that is slightly shaggy. The legs are medium long, thin and fine boned, ending in egg-shaped, small paws. The head is a rounded wedge shape, with a medium nose; the ears are large and heavily pointed, and the large, almond-shaped eyes are encircled by dark skin.

Regular brushing with a soft brush is recommended

Above: A Silver Sorrel Somali displaying the lithe, elongated body, bushy, fox-like tail and slightly arched back characteristic of the breed. The almond-shaped eyes are large and expressive, with a charming gaze.

Left: Ruddy Somali kittens (the most common variety) are very dark when first born. Their definitive coat colouring is slow to develop, only maturing fully when the cat is 18 months old. The adult coat is soft, long and silky, without being woolly, so grooming presents no problems.

Varieties: from left to right, Red, Ruddy and Blue.

KEY FACTS

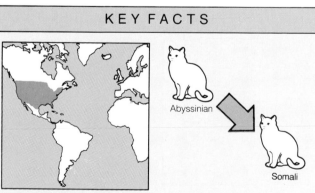

Abyssinian

Somali

Character: gentle, soft-voiced, can be shy and cautious, but is affectionate. Intelligent and athletic, enjoys access to outdoors and dislikes confined spaces.
Care: regular brushing will prevent matting. Diet should include plenty of meat and giblets.
Special problems: will overeat if allowed to. Cannot tolerate cold and requires special care in winter.

to prevent matting. The Somali's diet should include meat and giblets, although it will overeat these items whenever it gets the chance. The cat has no tolerance at all for cold and must be given special care in the winter months.

Kittens, generally two or three to a litter, are surprisingly small at birth. They also lack their true colouring and the long hair of the Somali; they will develop these sometime before their second year.

Standard faults in the breed are thin fur and undersized individuals.

CYMRIC

A LONG-HAIRED VERSION of the Manx, the Cymric first appeared in Canada in the 1960s in litters of strictly pedigreed cats that had no long-haired animals in their ancestry. The new cats were bred together, and the new breed held true.

The Cymric's predecessor, the Manx, is itself a genetic mutation first discovered on the Isle of Man, in the Irish Sea. The length of the tail, which is totally absent in the breed standard (referred to as "Rumpy"), actually can vary quite widely and in some individuals is only a bit shorter than normal cat tails. Some individuals have a remnant tail and these are dubbed "Stumpies," while those which have nearly full tails are called "Longies."

Some theories suggest that the Manx, and subsequently the Cymric, are actually the descendants of the Japanese Bobtail or a related breed that was somehow transported to this distant island half a world from its native land in the Far East. Other tales tell of invaders

KEY FACTS

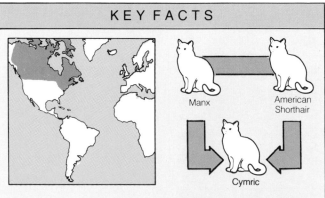

Manx   American Shorthair

Cymric

Character: lively, intelligent and affectionate. Tolerant even of dogs. Skilled mouser, enjoys outdoor exercise but is also home-loving.
Care: coat not prone to matting, but regular brushing is appreciated.
Special problems: prone to spina bifida; supplementing diet of breeding queens with vitamin B may help to reduce incidence.

Right: *Because the Isle of Man (origin of the Manx cat) lies off the coast of Wales, the longhaired version of the Manx was given the Celtic name for Welsh, Cymric. Like the Manx, the Cymric has a solid, compact body with a definite round rump. The hind legs are longer than the front ones, so that the body slopes forward.*

Varieties: from left to right, Blue Tortoiseshell Dilute Calico, Blue Smoke, Red Mackerel Tabby, Blue Cream and Tabby-Point.

that nipped the tails from the cats as a sort of victory symbol and of queens that habitually bit the tails from their offspring.

Cymrics are affectionate, intelligent cats, happiest when they are doing something. They have good mousing ability and enjoy time outdoors, but they are very comfortable in the home as well. They get along well with other animals, including dogs.

All colours and patterns are acceptable in the Cymric, which has a medium to long coat with a thick undercoat and shiny, smooth top hairs. The body has a stocky, muscular build. In the true breed standard, the end of the thumb should fit into the hollow that marks the spot where the tail should start. The overall body generally has an arched appearance, due to shorter than normal vertebrae.

The legs are short and thick, with the hindlegs longer than the forelegs. The paws are round and large. The head is round, with a short nose, strong chin, large, round eyes, and medium ears that are rounded at the tips.

The coat requires regular brushing, but it is easily groomed and very rarely mats. The Cymric is prone to spina bifida, the result of the same genes that affect the tail vertebrae.

Because the bodily features that give the breed its distinction are essentially genetic defects, the Cymric is a controversial breed. If it were introduced for recognition today, further breeding would probably be discouraged.

JAVANESE

WHEN THE BREEDING programmes for the Balinese were expanded to produce colours beyond those accepted for the Siamese in the United States (Seal-Point, Chocolate-Point, Lilac-Point and Blue-Point), the many different colours produced were grouped by Americans as a separate breed – the Javanese. In Britain all these pointed cats are known as Balinese. These varieties so far include the Cream-Point Javanese, with cream body with buff points; Red-Point

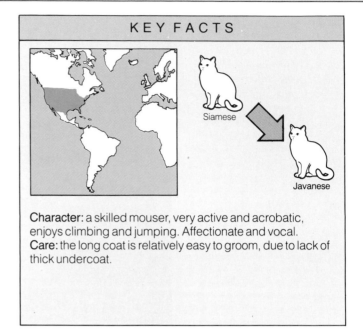

KEY FACTS

Siamese

Javanese

Character: a skilled mouser, very active and acrobatic, enjoys climbing and jumping. Affectionate and vocal.
Care: the long coat is relatively easy to groom, due to lack of thick undercoat.

Javanese, with cream body with light red points; Blue-Cream-Point Javanese, with white body with points patched in blue and cream; Tortoiseshell-Point Javanese, with off-white body with points patched in red and cream; Lilac-Cream-Point Javanese, with white body with points patched in pink-grey and cream; any of these colours in tabby markings (striped and spotted) on the points, which is called Lynx-Point in America.

The fur of the Javanese is long and silky. It lacks an undercoat and characteristic long-haired collar. The body is long and thin, with a medium-length, bushy tail. The legs are medium and thin, ending in round and large paws. The head is triangular, with a short nose, large, almond-shaped eyes that are slanted, and large, nontufted ears that are pointed at the tip.

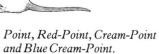

Varieties: *from left to right,* Point, Red-Point, Cream-Point
Tortoiseshell-Point, Tabby- *and Blue Cream-Point.*

Above: *A Red-Point Javanese kitten. The contrast between body and point colour is less pronounced in longhaired pointed cats than in shorthaired ones.*

Left: *Tortie, Red and Tabby varieties have been produced, using Colourpoint Shorthairs. Shown here is a Red-Point, with cream body and orange-red markings. The Javanese has the typically fine-boned, slender body of the Siamese, the long wedge-shaped head and the almond-shaped eyes. The coat is long and silky and the tail is well plumed.*

NORWEGIAN FOREST CAT

THE NORWEGIAN FOREST CAT is an ancient breed. Nordic mythology makes reference to the animal frequently, a theme that was picked up by writers of fables in the mid-1800s. They gave the cat enchanted qualities and often assigned it a dominant role in their plots. Recognized as a distinct breed in 1930, the cat was shown in Oslo, Norway, well before World War II.

While its features are markedly similar to the Maine Coon Cat of the northeastern United States, the two are separate breeds. The likeness is probably more a function of the rugged lifestyles of the ancestors of the two breeds rather than a common bloodline.

Comfortable around humans, the Norwegian Forest Cat must have space to roam and explore. It is happiest when involved in some activity, especially mousing, at which it is quite proficient.

The fur of the cat is thick and full, with a woolly undercoat for warmth and longer hairs for protection against inclement weather. The cat has a thick ruff. All colour variations are permitted.

As would be expected of a hardy cat from the North that is accustomed to outdoor life hunting its own food, the Norwegian Forest Cat's body is heavy and well muscled. Its legs are thick and strong. The paws are equipped with such able claws that the cat can climb rock walls. The tail is of medium length but thickly furred. The head is rounded with extremely large,

Left: This fine specimen shows off the abundant ruff and long, *bushy tail characteristic of the Norwegian Forest Cat.*

Varieties: top from left to right, Brown Tabby, Bicolour Blue-and-White, Tortoiseshell: bottom from left to right, Bicolour Black-and-White, Blue-Cream and Red Smoke.

KEY FACTS

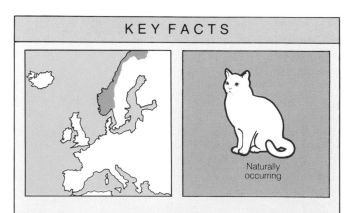

Naturally occurring

Character: a hardy outdoor breed, good hunter, extremely agile climber, intelligent and independent. Good-natured and enjoys human company.
Care: needs plenty of access to outdoors, varied diet of meat and fish. Coat needs only an occasional combing-through.

round eyes; it has noticeably heavy whiskers, a short nose and pointed, heavily tufted ears that are held erect.

Combing of the coat should be done only occasionally. The cat will shed once each year, retaining long-haired qualities only on its tail.

Meat and fish should be provided alternately as staples of the diet, but a Norwegian Forest Cat, given the roaming time that it needs, will often supply much of its own food.

Above: The Norwegian Forest Cat bears a strong resemblance to the American Maine Coon, though the two are unrelated. Bred of Scandinavian farm and feral stock, it is a hardy outdoor cat, equipped with a woolly undercoat for warmth and a long, water-resistant outer coat. The hind legs are slightly longer than the front ones.

TIFFANY

Burmese

Tiffany

Character: friendly, self-confident, humorous, likes attention. Adaptable to both indoor and outdoor life, enjoys travel. Long life expectancy.
Care: no special dietary requirements. Requires daily grooming to prevent matting.

A SHAGGY LONG-HAIRED mutation of the Burmese, the Tiffany retains the seal-brown colouring of the former. Kittens of this breed, which originated in the United States, generally do not display this long-haired quality at birth.

Like its Burmese ancestors, the Tiffany is loving of both its owner and new acquaintances, but demanding of praise, gentle attention and play time. It enjoys travel more than most cats, particularly when allowed to view the passing landscape through a car window. The Tiffany is an able mouser but adapts well to an indoor existence. It is generally quite a vocal cat throughout its life. It can live to a relatively old age, as long as 18 years.

The fur is long, thick and silky, hiding a muscular and strong body set on slender legs and large, egg-shaped paws. The tail is long and shaggy. The head appears round because of its ample covering of fur, although beneath it is triangular, like that of the Burmese. A strong chin is also hidden in fur. The eyes are wide and almond shaped, slanted slightly. They should be yellow-gold in colour. Ears are wide set, pointed at the tips and slightly tufted.

Daily brushing with a soft-bristle brush is needed to prevent matting. The cat generally has no special dietary requirements.

Below: The Tiffany is a beautiful cat with a long, silky coat. This one is a Cream, not yet recognized as a variety. The standard colour for the breed is a deep seal brown.

TURKISH VAN

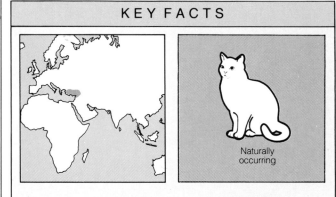

KEY FACTS

Naturally
occurring

Character: gentle, affectionate disposition. Enjoys water and will actively choose to bathe. Not very active, suited to indoor life.
Care: this breed has a hearty appetite, with no special dietary requirements. Daily grooming recommended. If handled regularly and gently from an early age, less prone to nervousness.

AN ANGORA CAT from the wintry region of Turkey's Lake Van, the Turkish Van was first imported into Great Britain in 1955 but not given official recognition until 1969. It has not yet been recognized in the United States.

Those members of this breed that have been born or raised near water generally enjoy swimming to an uncatlike degree. They can be quite good at it. As might be expected, they are easy to bathe.

The Turkish Van has been a house cat for many centuries, and as a result is affectionate towards the entire family. It will, however, select its own favourites, often individuals who share its peaceful nature. The breed is extremely intelligent, but prone to be less active and thus less demonstrative of that intelligence. Indoor life, with access to a small garden, suits the cat just fine.

There are only two varieties of the Turkish Van. The fur is usually white with chestnut red patches between the eyes and ears and on the tail, where the colour alternates in light and darker rings.

The body is muscular, full and long, but of delicate bone structure. The legs appear thicker than they are because of the heavy fur, and the feet are small and round.

Turkish Vans have a triangular face that appears framed by wide expanses of fur. The nose is long, the chin is flat and strong, and the eyes are small, rounded,

Above and right: *The "Van pattern" consists of red patches on the face and a red, ringed tail.*

An important accent is the white "blaze" down the forehead.

and close set. Ears are large, rounded, tufted, and pink on the inside.

Common standard faults include underdeveloped musculature, a truly round head, and markings on the body beyond those described above.

Daily brushing with a soft-bristle brush is recommended, as is periodic bathing. Meat is the staple of the diet, but the Turkish Van is not at all finicky.

To guard against a nervous nature in any individual Turkish Van, the cat must be handled gently but regularly from infancy. It is not a prolific breed, generally having litters of about four kittens.

RAGDOLL

THE RAGDOLL ORIGINATED in California and remains rare outside the United States.

This is a controversial breed, which relaxes completely when picked up or held. The resulting floppy "ragdoll" appearance gives the breed its name. The typical posture of the Ragdoll is flat on its side and completely relaxed.

Popular myth holds that the breed originated in the offspring of a female White Persian, injured when she was hit by a car. In this genetically unlikely scenario, those injuries led to a cat that cannot feel pain or face up to threats of any kind. The more scientifically based explanation for these unusual qualities in the Ragdoll is the heavily selective breeding that resulted in this cat.

It does in fact have an extremely high tolerance to pain, to the point that injuries can go unnoticed. It also has an overly mild nature. Therefore, the Ragdoll is best off when living completely indoors, a situation it seems happy to accept. The ideal owner is someone who is able to satisfy the cat's need for tranquility and

Above: Seal-Point Ragdoll kittens, in typically relaxed pose. This breed is still considered controversial, both its origin and its validity being in doubt.

Varieties: from left to right, Lilac-Point, Chocolate-Point and Mitted.

Below: The Ragdoll is similar in appearance to the Birman, except for its heavier body build and lack of tell-tale white "gloves". The colour points may be chocolate, as in this example, seal, blue or lilac.

some protection.

Varieties include the Bicolour Ragdoll, with a pale body, dark markings on the mask, ears and tail (seal, chocolate or lilac), and a white underside; Colourpoint Ragdoll, which has points in those same colours; and Mitted Ragdoll, which is the same as Colourpoint but with white front paws.

The fur is full and long, but not as long as many long-haired breeds. The body is long and solid, although it goes limp when picked up. It has medium legs, large, round paws and a long, medium tail. The head is a rounded wedge shape with a medium nose, fully developed cheeks, and small, round, blue eyes. Ears are medium, rounded at the tip, and tufted.

Common standard faults are an elongated muzzle, deformed tail, and crossed eyes.

Daily combing or brushing with the hands or a very light, soft instrument is recommended. Meat is the staple of the breed's diet.

KEY FACTS

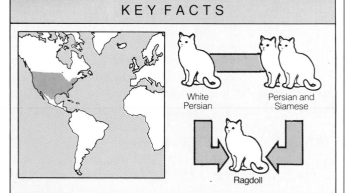

White Persian

Persian and Siamese

Ragdoll

Character: has an extremely docile temperament, enjoys the quiet life indoors. Goes limp when picked up.
Care: no special dietary requirements. Daily combing with the hands or a soft brush will keep the coat in good order.
Pedigree faults: elongated muzzle, deformed tail, crossed eyes.

BRITISH SHORTHAIR

Above: The White British Shorthair may have blue eyes, orange eyes, or one blue and one orange. The coat must be a pure white with no traces of yellow.

A NATURALLY OCCURRING type on the streets of Great Britain's cities and towns, the British Shorthair was refined into a recognized breed near the close of the 19th century. Breeders, who admired the intelligence and health of the cat, began to breed the "best".

The cat is generally healthy, strong, smart, and a skilled mouser. It can adapt to virtually all situations, but generally appears happiest when allowed some time outdoors. The British Shorthair quickly comes to love all who show it affection, especially children.

There are many varieties, sharing the same general physical characteristics. The fur is short but dense. The body is stocky and muscular with short, muscular legs and large, round paws. The tail is short, tapered, and rounded at the tip. The head is proportionately large and round, with a short nose and a well-defined chin. The eyes are round and large, and the ears are medium and rounded at the tips.

The White British Shorthair has three varieties: blue-eyed (often deaf), orange-eyed, and odd-eyed.

Black British Shorthairs are coal black with copper, gold, or orange eyes.

The Cream British Shorthair is extremely rare, especially perfect specimens, because of the tendency for tabby patterns to accompany its cream colour. The first of this variety appeared in tortoiseshell litters late in the 19th century, but it wasn't until 1920 that the intricacies of purposefully breeding for it were developed and the variety was officially recognized.

Blue British Shorthairs, with copper or orange eyes, appear identical to the Chartreux from France. Although some experts claim that the Chartreux is greyer in colour, the two are generally placed in the same class in U.S. and British shows. The Chartreux is said to have been bred by the Carthusian monks.

The Blue-Cream British Shorthair combines the blue and cream colours from which it was developed in a smoothly intermingled mix. It is almost always a female. The eyes are copper, orange or gold.

There are two tabby patterns. The Classic pattern has three stripes running along its back, a spiral on each flank, and two stripes across its chest like necklaces. Its forehead bears the letter "M." The Mackerel pattern resembles that of the tiger. It has more stripes than the Classic and no spirals on its flanks. Either pattern can occur in one of three varieties: brown, silver, or red.

Tortoiseshell British Shorthairs have black coats with patches of cream and red. A variety of this type is the Tortie-and-White, which also has white patches. The Smoke British Shorthair can occur in either black or blue topcoats over a white undercoat. Tipped British Shorthairs are the result of complicated selective breeding, giving a cat with a coat tipped in any recognized colour.

KEY FACTS

Best of non-pedigree cats

British Shorthair

Character: makes an excellent family pet, being intelligent, affectionate, easy to look after and less excitable than cats of foreign breeds.
Care: no special dietary requirements. Easy to groom.

Varieties: from left to right, Classic Pattern Red Tabby, Mackerel, Tortoiseshell-and-White, Cream, Blue and Blue-Cream.

Right: *The Cream is ideally pale in colour, free from any tabby markings, but this is very difficult to achieve in practice.*

BRITISH SPOTTED SHORTHAIR

THE BRITISH SPOTTED SHORTHAIR is another group of varieties of the British Shorthair, and as such shares the breed's common beginnings on the street. These cats were among those exhibited at the first shows in Great Britain.

Often referred to as "Spotties," these cats have the pattern of a Mackerel Tabby British Shorthair, but with the stripes broken up into spots. It is an extremely "wild" look, resembling the coats of some of the wild cats. For show standards, the spots should be as plentiful and distinct from one another as possible.

Spotting may be any colour accepted for other British Shorthairs, set against an appropriate ground colour, but red, brown and silver are most popular. The brown is light brown with black spots and copper, orange or gold eyes; the red is light red-brown spotted in darker red-brown with orange or copper eyes, and the silver is grey spotted in black with green or hazel eyes.

The physical characteristics of the British Shorthair continue in the British Spotted Shorthair. Short, dense fur covers a stocky, muscular body. The legs are muscular and end in large, round paws. The tail is short, tapered, and rounded at the tip. The head is proportionally large and round, with a short nose and a well-defined chin. The eyes are round and large, and the ears are medium and rounded at the tips.

The other characteristics of the British Shorthair, developed when it was the cat of the streets, are also carried over. The British Spotted Shorthair is healthy, strong and smart. It is a skilled mouser. It also can adapt to virtually all situations, but generally appears happiest when allowed some time outdoors.

The fur should be rubbed occasionally with a gloved hand. Diet is not restricted, although meat should form the daily foundation.

Common standard faults are irregular noses and tails, and long-haired or shaggy coats.

Varieties: from left to right, Silver, Red, Brown and Blue.

Left: The show standard for British Spotted Shorthairs (this one is a Silver Tabby) requires that the spots are as numerous and as clearly defined as possible, with spots or broken rings on the tail. The presence of white in the coat is regarded as a fault. Eye colour should correspond to the coat colour.

KEY FACTS

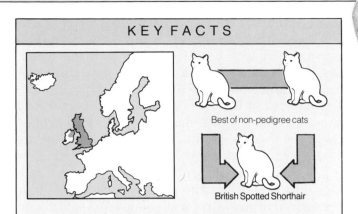

Best of non-pedigree cats

British Spotted Shorthair

Character: as with the British Shorthair, it is healthy, hardy and independent. A skilled mouser, home-loving but also enjoys roaming outdoors. Affectionate and good with children.

Care: no special dietary requirements. Groom by rubbing occasionally with a gloved hand.

Pedigree faults: irregular nose or tail, long or shaggy coat.

Left: *This example has a well proportioned body and excellent spotted markings.*

BRITISH BICOLOUR SHORTHAIR

MANY PETS APPEAR to be of this variety grouping of the British Shorthair, but in reality the true pedigree is far from common. In pedigrees the white patches should make up one third and not more of the coat. A symmetrical arrangement is preferred with patches of colour on the top of the head, ears, cheeks, back, tail, legs and flanks.

The common, demanding life on the streets of the breed's ancestors serves the cats well. They are generally healthy, strong and smart. Skilled mousers, they are able to fend for themselves. They adapt to virtually all situations, but are generally active and happy in homes that allow them some time outdoors. They are affectionate to everyone who treats them well

and tolerant and loving towards children.

There are four varieties, sharing the same general physical characteristics. The fur is short but dense. The body is stocky and muscular with short, muscular legs and large, round paws. The tail is short, tapered, and rounded at the tip. The head is proportionately large and round, with a short nose and a well-defined chin. The eyes are round and large, and the ears are medium and rounded at the tips.

The four colours recognized are British Cream-and-White Bicolour Shorthair, British Orange-and-White Bicolour Shorthair, British Black-and-White Bicolour Shorthair, and British Blue-and-White Bicolour Shorthair. All have copper or orange eyes.

Left: A Black-and-White Bicolour. The show standard for Bicolours requires copper or orange eyes with no green rims.

Occasional rubbing with a gloved hand is recommended to keep the fur in its prime. Meat is the staple for a generally wide-ranging, non-restrictive diet.

Hair that is too long or shaggy, and irregular noses or tails are common standard faults of the breed.

Varieties: from left to right, Cream-and-White, Orange-

and-White, Black-and-White and Blue-and-White.

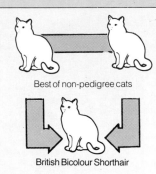

KEY FACTS

Best of non-pedigree cats

British Bicolour Shorthair

Character: as with the British Shorthair, it is healthy, hardy and independent. A skilled mouser, home-loving but also enjoys roaming outdoors. Affectionate and good with children.

Care: no special dietary requirements. Groom by rubbing occasionally with a gloved hand.

Pedigree faults: irregular nose or tail, long or shaggy coat.

Left: In terms of character and temperament, the British Shorthair has much in common with its distant relative, the non-pedigree domestic cat; it is strong, robust, intelligent and a skilled hunter, while also affectionate and suited to domestic life. In terms of appearance, however, the pedigree cat wins hands down, with its compact, well proportioned body, deep, broad chest, massive, round head and fur that is dense and rich in colour. The standard for Bicolours requires that the colour is well defined and evenly distributed. Not more than two-thirds of the cat's coat should be coloured, and not more than half should be white. This example is a Blue-and-White Bicolour.

MANX

THE TRUE ORIGINS of this unusual breed are steeped in claims, counterclaims, legend, and folktale. The total lack of a tail is attributed to everything from Noah catching the latecomer cat's tail in the door of the Ark, to mother cats deliberately biting off the tails of their kittens to prevent them from future pain at the hands of invading armies, who hung the tails they captured from their shields like medals.

The Phoenicians, noted seafaring merchants of the ancient world, are sometimes credited with spreading the breed from the Far East to the Isle of Man, in the Irish Sea. If this tale were true, then the Manx would have to be a mutation or adaptation of something akin to the Japanese Bobtail.

A more likely origin of the Manx was on galleons of the Spanish Armada. Some tailless cats (there were always rat-control cats aboard the ships) the result of a

mutation, made their way ashore when some of the Spanish ships sank near the Isle of Man in the late 1500s. There, isolated from other breeds, their tailless quality was passed on to new generations. Later, breeders built on this beginning to develop the breed by careful crossing with tailed cats.

Whatever their beginnings, the residents of the Isle of Man are quite proud of their distinctive cat, so much so that they have minted a coin in its likeness.

The Manx is an even-tempered, loving, intelligent breed. It is comfortable with anyone who comes into the home, the place where the cat prefers to spend all of its time. Despite this indoor preference, the Manx is an extremely active breed, happiest when involved in some activity, and an able mouser with lightning-quick reflexes. It needs play as part of its daily routine.

The breed is recognized in any shorthair coat colour

KEY FACTS

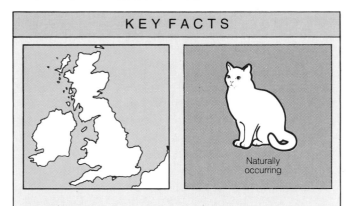

Naturally
occurring

Character: friendly, intelligent, easy to train. Home-loving, but also a good hunter, with quick reflexes. Known for its longevity.
Care: no special dietary requirements. Gentle brushing will maintain silkiness of the fur.
Special problems: spina bifida is relatively common; raising the level of vitamin B in the diet of pregnant queens is recommended to counteract this.

Varieties: from left to right, White with Blue Eyes, Blue-Cream, Black, Tortoiseshell and Bicolour Blue.

Below: The rumpy Manx is completely tailless. At the point where the tail should begin there is a small hollow, sometimes covered with a tuft of hair.

Above: In the Manx the hind legs are longer than the forelegs, so that the cat's walk resembles a rabbit's hopping gait.

or pattern; the eye colour should complement the coat. The mark of a true pedigree is a hollow where the base of the tail should be that will accommodate the end of a thumb. These tailless cats are referred to as "Rumpy," while those with remnant tails are known as "Stumpy."

The fur is short and dense. The body is stocky and muscular with powerful legs; the forelegs are shorter than the hindlegs. The head is egg shaped and broad, with a short nose, large, round eyes, and a well-developed chin. The ears are medium in size and rounded at the tips.

Frequent, gentle brushing with a soft-bristle brush is recommended to maintain the silky quality of the fur. The Manx is not at all finicky in its diet.

Breeding is a problem with this cat. Mating two tailless cats results in malformed kittens that die before birth or soon after. Therefore, tailless individuals should be bred with those with tails.

Common standard faults are a small head, long tail, and lack of an undercoat.

The Manx is one of only two tailless breeds. The other is the Cymric, actually a long-haired mutation of the Manx that first appeared in the 1960s in Canada.

AMERICAN SHORTHAIR

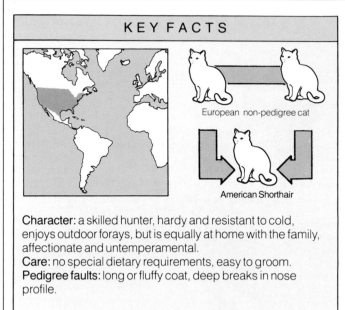
LIKE ITS BRITISH cousin and partial ancestor, the American Shorthair is very much a cat of the streets, the barnyards and the countryside. It was brought to North America on the same ships that brought the European settlers, to protect the ship's stores from mice and rats. Once ashore they interbred and adapted to a new lifestyle and environment.

The first officially recognized individual of the breed was Buster Brown, a cross between British Shorthairs and the emerging American cats; that was in 1904.

As happened with the British Shorthair, breeders quickly began to breed from the best of the naturally occurring cats.

Another characteristic the American Shorthair shares with its British counterpart is its hardy, healthy nature. Even larger and more muscular than the British Shorthair, this American cat epitomizes the pioneer spirit of the nation. It is a bold, inquisitive cat with a "working" past that needs outside spaces to roam. Always ready to do something, anything, the American Shorthair is happiest when active.

The breed will show affection to the entire family and friends, as long as it receives respect in return. It also demands praise when returning from a successful hunt with dead prey in tow.

Befitting a cat that originated in the outdoors, the fur is thick and dense, the body is athletic and strong, the legs are medium and powerful with large, round paws. The head is egg shaped (with the more pointed ends on the sides of the head) with large, round eyes and a well-developed muzzle. The ears are medium in size, rounded at the tips, and lightly tufted.

There is a large number of varieties: White, with white coat, no markings, and blue, gold or odd eyes; Black, with black coat, no markings, and gold eyes; Blue, with blue-grey coat, no markings, and gold eyes; Red, with red-brown coat, no markings, and gold eyes; Cream, with buff coat, no markings, and gold eyes; Bicolour, with white coat with blue, black, red or cream patches and gold eyes; Shaded Silver, with white undercoat with grey-tipped markings and green eyes.

Brown Tabby, with brown coat with black Classic or Mackerel pattern and gold eyes; Red Tabby, with red coat with darker red Classic or Mackerel pattern and gold eyes; Silver Tabby, with grey coat with black Classic or Mackerel pattern and green eyes; Blue Tabby, with bluish coat with dark grey Classic or Mackerel pattern and gold eyes; Cream Tabby, with cream coat with darker cream Classic or Mackerel pattern and gold eyes; Cameo Tabby, with white coat with red Classic or Mackerel pattern and gold eyes;

Above: The American Shorthair is slightly heavier than its British cousins, with longer legs and neck and a narrower head. This mother and kitten are Shaded Silvers.

Varieties: top from left to right, White odd-eyed, Black with gold eyes, Cream with orange eyes: *bottom from left to right, Silver Tabby, Red Bicolour, and Shaded Silver.*

Patched Tabby, with silver, brown or blue coat with black or light silver Classic or Mackerel pattern, red or cream patches and gold eyes.

Chinchilla, with white undercoat with black tipping and green or blue-green eyes; Shell Cameo, with white undercoat with red tipping and gold eyes; Shaded Cameo, with white undercoat with longer red tips than the Shell Cameo and gold eyes; Cameo Smoke, with white undercoat with red tipping and gold eyes.

Blue Smoke, with white undercoat with blue tipping and gold eyes; Black Smoke, with white undercoat with black tipping and gold eyes; Blue-Cream, with bluish coat with cream patches and gold eyes; Tortoiseshell, with black with cream and red patches and gold eyes; Tortoiseshell Smoke, with white undercoat with black, red, and cream tipping in tortoiseshell pattern and gold eyes; Calico, white with red and black patches and gold eyes.

AMERICAN WIREHAIR

Right: At first glance, the American Wirehair looks like any other shorthaired cat. But on closer inspection, the hair has an unusual appearance, as if crimped with tongs; it feels wiry and coarse to the touch, and springs back when stroked. This example is a Calico.

Varieties: from left to right, Red, Brown Tabby, Calico, Blue-Cream and Shaded Cameo.

A "PERMED" VERSION of the American Shorthair from which it sprang, the American Wirehair has all the same features as its predecessor but with curly or hooked hair. This coat has a rough texture and springs back when touched.

The breed is among the newer ones. Its first example, a white-and-red tom named Adam, was produced as a mutation in a litter of American Shorthairs in 1966 in Vernon, New York. A breeder mated Adam to a littermate and produced two similarly wire-haired kittens, thus giving the breed its start. The name was borrowed from the Wirehaired Terrier.

The wire-haired feature is a dominant characteristic, which means that wire-haired kittens will be born in the first generation of a mating between a Wirehair and an "ordinary" short-hair.

Similarly wire-haired cats appeared naturally on the streets of London during World War II, making their homes in the bombed-out ruins of the city. Some were

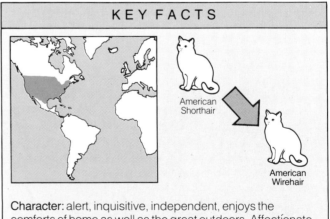

KEY FACTS

American Shorthair

American Wirehair

Character: alert, inquisitive, independent, enjoys the comforts of home as well as the great outdoors. Affectionate and loving. Both sexes make devoted parents.
Care: no special dietary requirements. Occasional brushing is recommended.
Pedigree faults: long or fluffy coat, deformed tail, deep breaks in nose profile.

Above: *This Tabby-and-White shows the playful, inquisitive and intelligent character of the Wirehair.*

exhibited in cat shows, but the trait was not bred through after the initial interest and the breed is not exhibited in Britain.

Like its progenitor, the American Wirehair is even-tempered, smart, and happiest when doing something. It shows interest in nearly everything around it and is affectionate towards the entire family, although it appreciates respect and tranquility. The cat enjoys the comforts of home but also needs to roam open spaces.

Varieties are similar to the American Shorthair, with the exception of the patched tabby pattern: White, Black, Blue, Red, Cream, Bicolour, Shaded Silver, Brown Tabby, Red Tabby, Silver Tabby, Blue Tabby, Cream Tabby, Cameo Tabby, Chinchilla, Shell Cameo, Shaded Cameo, Cameo Smoke, Blue Smoke, Black Smoke, Blue-Cream, Tortoiseshell, Tortoiseshell Smoke, and Calico. (See American Shorthair.)

The fur of the American Wirehair is dense, curly, woolly and coarse. The body is athletic and powerful, set on medium-sized legs that are likewise powerful and large, with round paws. The tail is long, straight, and ends in a rounded point. The head is egg shaped with a square muzzle; there is a well-developed chin and wide-set, large, round eyes with a slight slant. The ears are medium and rounded at the tips. Males are larger than females. Like the American Shorthair, this breed make excellent parents.

Occasional brushing with a soft-bristle brush and combing in moderation is recommended. Diet should be meat based, although the Wirehair is not finicky.

Common standard faults are fur that is too long or soft, deformed tail, and too hard a break in the nose.

EXOTIC SHORTHAIR

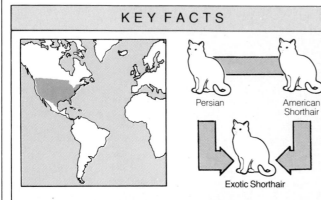

KEY FACTS

Persian

American Shorthair

Exotic Shorthair

Character: combines the placid, affectionate nature of the Persian with the playful inquisitiveness of the American Shorthair; makes an ideal family pet.
Care: gentle brushing will keep the coat in good condition. Likes a varied diet of meat, cooked vegetables and giblets.
Pedigree faults: flat or uneven coat, short or deformed tail, head that is too small, eyes that contrast with coat colouring.

ANOTHER DESCENDANT OF the American Shorthair is the Exotic Shorthair, although this is a man-made breed rather than a natural mutation. Through selective breeding of Persians and American Shorthairs in the 1960s, this new breed was created to carry the dignified character of the Persian but with the shorter, easier-to-care-for coat of the American Shorthair. For a brief period Burmese were also used in the breeding, but they soon fell from favour.

The Exotic Shorthair inherited portions of its temperament from both parental lines. It is calm, less active, and affectionate to the whole family like the Persian and playful, inquisitive, and an able mouser like the American Shorthair. This new breed also forms an attachment to its home.

All varieties of both the Persians and the American Shorthairs are acceptable, including: White, Black, Cream, Red, Blue, Blue-Cream, Chinchilla, Shaded Silver, Red Shell Cameo, Red Shaded Cameo, Red

Varieties: from left to right, Black, Blue Smoke, Cream, Silver Tabby and Cameo Tortoiseshell.

Right: The Exotic Shorthair is the result of selective breeding between American Shorthairs and the best Persians. The cat is Persian in type, with a cobby body and round, massive head, but the dense, soft coat is shorter and easier to groom than that of a Longhair.

Right: A Black Smoke Exotic Shorthair. The eyes are a distinctive feature of this breed, being huge and wideset, with a sweet expression. These cats are very popular in the United States, and are becoming increasingly popular in Britain.

Smoke Cameo, Cream Shell Cameo, Cream Shaded Cameo, Cream Smoke Cameo, Cameo Tortie, Cameo Tabby, Black Smoke, Blue Smoke, Smoke Tortoiseshell, Bicolour, Red Tabby, Brown Tabby, Silver Tabby, Blue Tabby, Cream Tabby, Patched Tabby, Tortoiseshell and Calico. Eye colouring must complement coat colouring. For explanations of these, see the sections on Longhairs and American Shorthairs.

The fur is dense and plush but of medium length. The body is short and low-set, with short, thick legs and large, round paws. The tail is short and bushy, but not as bushy as that of the Persian. The head is round with a short nose; there are fully developed cheeks and large, round eyes. The ears are small, wide set, and pointed at the tips.

The coat is easily cared for with gentle brushing. A diet of meat, giblets and some cooked vegetables must be restricted in quantity to avoid weight problems.

Litters of four are the average. The kittens are generally much darker than their parents, gaining their true colours only at maturity.

Common standard faults are a short or deformed tail, eyes that contrast with the coat colouring, and a head that is too small.

SIAMESE

IF THERE IS one breed of cat that is instantly recognizable by nearly everyone, including nonenthusiasts, it must be the Siamese. No other colouring is as universally familiar as the classic Seal-Point Siamese.

The breed started quite some time ago in the Far East. Already in the late 16th century, Siamese cats were revered pets around the royal court in Siam, but it probably saw its origins in some as yet unidentified wild breed even further to the east.

Its coming to Great Britain and the United States is quite recent by comparison. The first Siamese appeared in British shows in the early 1870s, gifts from the King of Siam to the British Consul-General in Bangkok. It was 1890 before the cats made their way to the United States, again as gifts from the King, this time to an American acquaintance.

The Siamese was the "in" cat during the early 1900s, creating such a demand that breeders began turning them out in great numbers with little regard for the animals themselves. The process, complete with much inbreeding, took its toll. The Siamese had become a weak, sickly breed and was nearing extinction when breeders finally recognized the threat and began exercising more care.

An extrovert in every sense of the word, the Siamese

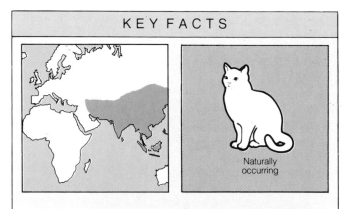

KEY FACTS

Naturally occurring

Character: very strong personality, demands a lot but gives a lot in return. Highly intelligent, can be trained to walk with harness and leash. Highly vocal, given to fits of jealousy.
Care: brush daily to remove dead hairs. Varied diet of meat, fish and cooked vegetables, plus vitamin supplements.
Pedigree faults: non-blue eyes, malformed tail or chin, weak legs, white feet.

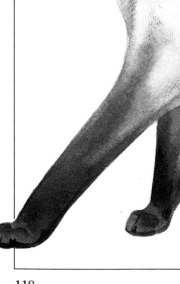

Left: The original Siamese is the Seal-Point variety. The mask, ears, legs, feet and tail are a rich, dark colour in contrast to the rest of body, which is beige or light fawn. The eyes are an intense blue.

America: Seal-Point, with beige coat with seal-brown points; Chocolate-Point, with snow white coat with milk-chocolate points; Blue-Point, with snow white coat with grey points; Lilac-Point, with snow white coat with pink-grey points. In Great Britain, the Tabby-Points, Tortie-Tabby-Points, Tortie-Points (in all their colours), Red-Points, and Cream-Points are also officially recognized as Siamese, but in America these are classed as a separate breed: the Colorpoint Shorthairs.

The fur of the Siamese is short, very soft, and exceedingly fine. The body is thin and slender, with long, thin legs and small, egg-shaped paws. The head is large and triangular, with medium-sized, almond-shaped eyes that are slanted; it has a pointed muzzle. The ears are large and pointed at the tips.

Common standard faults are nonblue eyes, spotting on the underside, malformed tail, malformed chin, weak legs and white feet.

Daily brushing with a medium-hard brush is recommended to remove dead hairs, especially during shedding periods. An exclusively meat diet tends to damage the light colours of the coat, so fish and cooked vegetables should be used alternately with meat. Vitamin supplements are also advisable.

loves to have visitors into its home, to the point of sometimes being intrusive. It is free with its affection, and if given the attention it demands will be a dedicated companion. The Siamese can also be quite jealous of other cats and even humans. It is one of the few cats that can be trained to walk on a leash like a dog.

Its personality is also subject to unpredictable, wide swings, from a happy, playful cat one day, to a moody, sulking animal the next. The Siamese is one of our more vocal breeds, making frequent use of a loud voice that proves difficult to ignore.

There are only four recognized breeds in North

Varieties: from left to right, Chocolate-Point, Blue-Point, Lilac-Point and Seal-Point.

Right: Another traditional variety, the Blue-Point's colour points are grey, and the coat is ice white.

COLORPOINT SHORTHAIR

IN GREAT BRITAIN the varieties of this breed are officially considered Siamese cats, but in the United States they are classified as a separate breed because of the more recent non-Siamese side of their lineage.

Colorpoint Shorthairs are produced by mating Siamese cats with other breeds, such as Abyssinians, to bring new colours and patterns to the traditional Siamese points.

The results to date include Red-Point, white coat with red-brown points; Cream-Point, white coat with cream points; Seal-Lynx-Point, fawn coat with brown tabby points; Chocolate-Lynx-Point, white coat with brown tabby points; Blue-Lynx-Point, blue-white coat with grey tabby points; Lilac-Lynx-Point, white coat with pink-grey tabby points; Red-Lynx-Point, white coat with red-brown tabby points; Seal-Tortie-Point, fawn coat with brown points marked with cream and red; Chocolate-Tortie-Point, white coat with brown points marked with cream; Blue-Tortie-Point, blue-white coat with grey points marked with cream; Lilac-Tortie-Point, white coat with pink-grey points marked with cream.

Other than the colouring, the Colorpoint Shorthair carries through the characteristics of the Siamese. It's an extrovert that enjoys all people who give it the attention it demands. It can become a dedicated companion and will be taught to walk on a leash like a dog. The Colorpoint Shorthair also can become jealous of all creatures that compete with it for attention. It has the same loud voice as the Siamese and is just as willing to use it.

The fur is Siamese-like: short, soft and fine. The body is thin and slender, with long, thin legs and small, egg-shaped paws. The head is large and triangular, with medium-sized, almond-shaped eyes that are slanted, and it has a pointed muzzle. The ears are large and pointed at the tips.

Common standard faults are nonblue eyes, spotting on the underside, malformed tail, malformed chin, weak legs and white feet.

Daily brushing with a medium-hard brush is recommended to remove dead hairs, especially during shedding periods. An exclusively meat diet tends to damage the light colours of the coat, so fish and cooked vegetables should be used alternately with meat. Vitamin supplements are also advisable, particularly in infancy.

Left: *Seemingly active even in repose, the Colorpoint Shorthair shares the same acrobatic traits and lively personality as the Siamese. Shown here is a Cream-Point, with white coat and points of a delicate apricot shade.*

Below: This Red-Point shows off the long, svelte body, fine legs and wedge-shaped head so admired in the breed. Red-Points inevitably show some tabby markings.

KEY FACTS

Siamese → American Shorthair → Colorpoint Shorthair

Character: similar to the Siamese. Highly intelligent and extrovert, enjoys human company and will walk on a leash. Has a long life expectancy.
Care: daily grooming to remove dead hairs, especially during shedding periods. Fish and cooked vegetables should be given as well as meat.
Pedigree faults: non-blue eyes, spotting on the underside, malformed tail or chin, weak legs, white feet.

Varieties: top from left to right, Cream, Lynx-Point, Red-Lynx-Point: bottom from left to right, Chocolate Tortoiseshell-Point, Lilac Tortoiseshell-Point and Blue Tortoiseshell-Point.

RUSSIAN BLUE

been known as the Maltese and the Spanish Blue.

The Russian Blue is very quiet and shy, and does best when living with people that share these traits. It is ever-eager to show its affection and to please its owners. The indoor life is preferred, and although the cat's ancestry comes from a cold climate, it will seek warm spots in the house and spend many winter hours there.

A white variety was produced for a time in Great Britain, but dropped from most breeding efforts due to lack of interest. It is now very rare.

The fur of the Russian Blue is like that of a plush-covered toy. A heavy undercoat gives the fur the sheen of mink. Colour ranges through all grey shades, although a blue-grey colour is what originally gave the cat its current name.

The body is long, slender and muscular, with a long tail. The legs are thin, with small, round paws. The hindlegs are slightly longer than the forelegs. The head is egg shaped with a medium nose, well-developed muzzle and medium-sized, oval eyes. The ears are large and rounded at the tips, with skin that is almost transparent.

Regular brushing is recommended, and the hair should be brushed so that it remains upright and does not flatten. The Russian Blue needs a varied diet including meat, giblets and cooked vegetables.

As this breed tends to deteriorate quickly, top-quality specimens are generally produced only by two pure parents. Both sexes are excellent feline parents.

Common standard faults are a head that is too wide, white hairs or spots, and overweight.

Above: Elegant and graceful in outline, the Russian Blue resembles the Egyptian cat of the *Pharaohs with its long, slim legs, elongated neck and tail and erect ears.*

THIS BREED PROBABLY originated in the Russian port city of Archangel and was brought into Great Britain in the late 1800s aboard a Russian merchant ship. Similar cats are still found in that region today. But there remains confusion about the Russian Blue because of the many aliases it has travelled under. At first it was known as the Archangel Blue. The current name took hold in the 1940s. At various times the cat has also

KEY FACTS

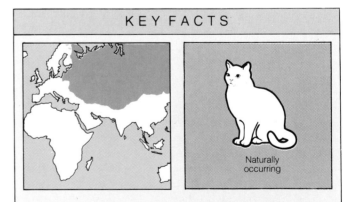

Naturally occurring

Character: quiet, shy, very affectionate and devoted to its owners. Well suited to indoor life. Both sexes make good parents.
Care: regular brushing to maintain a healthy coat; take care not to flatten the coat if exhibiting the cat. Needs a varied diet with meat, giblets and cooked vegetables.
Pedigree faults: uneven coat, too wide a head, overweight.

Right: The head of the Russian Blue is distinctive in shape, with prominent whisker pads and a strong chin. The ears are large and pointed, and set vertically on the head, and the eyes are a vivid green and wide-set.

KORAT

THE KORAT IS not a common breed. It is rare even in its native land of Thailand. It's an ancient breed with a long history. Originating in the province of Korat (Si-Sawat in the local language), the cat was given the same name as the land. The name loosely translates into "good fortune," and a pair of the cats was always among the traditional wedding gifts to Thai brides. The cats were also given to nobility as testimony of their subjects' loyalty and reverence toward them.

The Korat's affectionate, quiet nature is befitting of such an animal. The breed is also inquisitive by nature, knowledgeable about everything in its environment. The Korat prefers to be totally indoors; street noises and even a busy household are extremely upsetting to the animal. However, it remains playful with its human owners throughout its life. It is one of the very few breeds that seems to delight in learning and performing repetitive tricks on command. On the other hand, it is severely combative toward any strange cats brought into the home.

The first Korats were brought into the United States in 1959. Official recognition came in 1966, and the breed entered Great Britain in 1972. There are no varieties of the Korat beyond the solid silver-blue.

Above: A rare beauty, the Korat is blessed with a unique coat of blue with a silvery sheen. The round green eyes are huge and luminous.

Above: *The Korat is one of the "good luck" cats of Thailand, and an ancient poem praises its* coat with "roots that are clouds and points that are silver".

The fur is short, thick and silky, with no undercoat. The body is stocky and muscular, with a medium-length tail that ends in a point. The legs are medium and strong, ending in small, egg-shaped paws. The head has a definite heart shape to it, with a short nose but overall pronounced muzzle. Eyes are large, round, prominent and green or amber-green. Ears are very large and rounded at the points.

A daily rubbing with a gloved hand is recommended, as are precautions against viral infections in the respiratory system. The Korat does quite well on a meat-based diet.

Both sexes make very devoted, playful and loving parents. Kittens do not reach their full potential colouring until about two years of age.

KEY FACTS

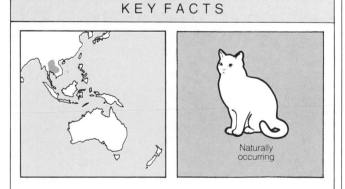

Naturally occurring

Character: quiet and affectionate, makes an intelligent and loving pet. Playful, inquisitive, likes to perform tricks. Prefers indoor life and is easily upset by loud noises.
Care: groom by rubbing daily with a gloved hand. Vaccination against viral infections is vital.
Special problems: not a hardy breed; prone to chills and respiratory infections in cooler climates.

ABYSSINIAN

KEY FACTS

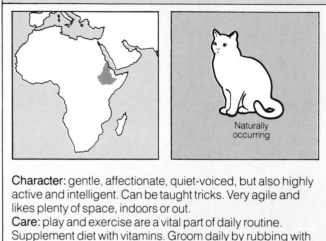

Naturally
occurring

Character: gentle, affectionate, quiet-voiced, but also highly active and intelligent. Can be taught tricks. Very agile and likes plenty of space, indoors or out.
Care: play and exercise are a vital part of daily routine. Supplement diet with vitamins. Groom daily by rubbing with a gloved hand.

COMMON BELIEF HOLDS that the Abyssinian is the direct descendant of the sacred Temple cats of ancient Egypt, the models for the Egyptian goddess Bast. Comparisons of the modern cat to mummified remains from ancient tombs and to painted frescoes in the tombs seem to support that belief.

The foundation cats are said to have been brought to Great Britain in the 1860s by soldiers returning from Abyssinia, and the popularity of the new breed grew rapidly. However, during the two world wars the breed was almost lost due to lack of adequate food, and in the 1960s it was threatened by widespread feline leukaemia. It has recovered from those hard times and is again a popular breed, especially in the States.

Abyssinians are intelligent, inquisitive animals

Varieties: *from left to right,*
Ruddy, Red and Blue.

and will learn tricks quickly. They do, however, cherish their freedom and will become quite restless if totally confined indoors. They are excellent climbers and, as with any display of their abilities, expect to be praised for it. Even indoors they are happiest when involved in some activity. Above all breeds, the Abyssinians need play with their owners as part of their daily routine. If play is neglected they will become

sullen and isolate themselves, even to the extent of abandoning their home.

They can require some time to become attached to their owners, but will respond to gentle and soft-spoken attention. They also show a tendency to attach themselves to one member of the family in particular.

There are three varieties in America: Ruddy, brown coat ticked with bands of darker brown; Red, red-brown coat ticked with light brown; and Blue, blue-grey ticked with deeper blue. In Britain, Chocolate, Lilac, Fawn, Silver, Sorrel/Silver and Blue/Silver are also known. Each variety shows a coat that is a gentle blend of shading; this is because each hair is lighter at the root and darker at the tip.

The body is long and slender with long, slender legs, small, egg-shaped paws, and a long, tapered tail. The head is rounded with a medium nose; it has large, almond-shaped eyes that are slanted and large ears that are pointed at the tips. Common standard faults are a stocky body, spots and markings on the body, and white on the neck.

Meat, in any form, is the favoured food of the Abyssinian. It will overeat meat whenever it gets the chance. Vitamin supplements are recommended, particularly while the cat is growing. The coat should be brushed and rubbed with a gloved hand every day.

Pregnant females need special attention because they remain quite active throughout their pregnancy and falls are common. Kittens – three or four in the typical litter – begin life with dark markings that they lose after a few months.

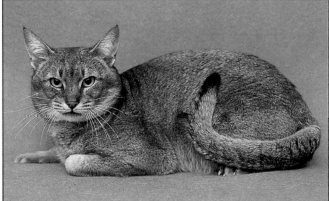

Above and right: The Abyssinian is a very striking cat, with its long and slender body, prominent, erect ears and huge eyes, which have been described as "the biggest, most innocent eyes in the world". The traditional form, shown here, is known as ruddy in the United States and normal or usual in Britain. It is a rich golden brown with dark brown or black ticking, and the tip of the tail and the hind legs are dark brown or black. Abyssinians make ideal companions, being gentle, quiet-voiced and very affectionate.

FOREIGN OR ORIENTAL SHORTHAIR

THE COLOURPOINT CATS that we so instantly and so easily identify as Siamese are in fact only one part of that Far East breed. In their native Thailand (Siam), the cats also appear in many solid colour variations.

Such variations, which were introduced in the 1970s in the United States, are known as the Oriental Shorthair.

The same cats in Great Britain and Europe are known as Foreign. Each colour is considered its own breed and is referred to as such: for example, Foreign Red and Foreign Ebony. The name originated in the 1920s, when breeders of the solid-coloured animals saw their animals excluded from Siamese categories and created the new breed catagories to include their cats.

The Foreign or Oriental Shorthair has the personality of the Siamese. It's a lively and energetic cat, with intense curiosity about everything around it. Lots of

Below: The Foreign Shorthair is a solid-coloured Siamese. The White has a pure-white coat and *brilliant blue or green eyes. The body is long, slender and fine-boned.*

play and exercise must be part of the cat's daily routine for it to be truly happy. Like the Siamese, the Foreign Shorthair can be trained to walk on a leash.

The various colours are divided into five classes: Solid, Shaded, Smoke, Tabby and Bi-(Parti) Colour.

Solid: White, with white coat and blue, green or yellow eyes; Ebony, with black coat and green or yellow eyes; Red, with red-brown coat and green or yellow eyes; Lilac (Lavender), with pink-grey coat and green or yellow eyes; Chestnut, with brown coat and green eyes; Blue, with grey coat and green or yellow eyes.

Shaded: Cameo, with white undercoat tipped with red; Silver, with white undercoat tipped with black, blue, brown, or pink-grey.

Smoke (tipped more heavily than the Shaded): Black Smoke, with white undercoat tipped with black; Blue Smoke, with white undercoat tipped with grey; Chestnut Smoke, with white undercoat tipped with brown; Lilac (Lavender) Smoke, with white undercoat tipped with pink-grey; Cameo Smoke, with white undercoat tipped with red-brown.

Tabby: Classic, Mackerel, Spotted, or Ticked, in any of the Tabby colours. Also Ebony Tabby, with brown coat with black markings; Silver Tabby, with silver coat with black markings; Red Tabby, with brown-red coat with darker markings; Cameo Tabby, with white coat with red-brown markings; Cream Tabby, with cream coat with buff markings; Chestnut Tabby, with light brown coat with brown markings; Blue Tabby, with blue-white coat with grey markings; Lilac (Lavender) Tabby, with grey coat with pink-grey markings.

Bi-Colour (Patched): Blue-Cream, with grey coat with cream patches; Lavender-Cream, with grey coat with cream patches; Tortoiseshell, with black coat with red and cream patches; Chestnut-Tortie, with brown coat with red and cream patches.

The fur of the Foreign Shorthair, like that of the Siamese, is short, very soft, and exceedingly fine. The body is thin and slender, with long, thin legs and small, egg-shaped paws. The head is large and triangular,

Varieties: from left to right, Black Solid with green eyes, Cameo Shaded, Chestnut Smoke, Chestnut Tabby, and Tortoiseshell.

with medium-sized, almond-shaped eyes that are slanted; it has a pointed muzzle. The ears are large and pointed at the tips.

Daily brushing with a medium-hard brush is recommended to remove dead hairs, especially during shedding periods. An exclusively meat diet tends to damage the light colours of the coat, so fish and cooked vegetables should be used alternately with meat.

KEY FACTS

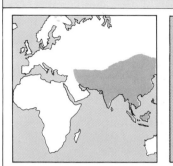 

Naturally occurring

Character: identical to that of the Siamese. Demands and gives total devotion. Enjoys travel and will walk on a leash Very active and highly vocal.

Care: needs lots of play and exercise, daily grooming to remove dead hairs, varied diet of meat, fish and cooked vegetables, plus multivitamins.

Above: *The Ebony Oriental Shorthair, or Foreign Black, is svelte and stylish, its intense green eyes accentuated by the glossy, jet-black coat.*

HAVANA

ALTHOUGH ITS NAME conjures up a vision of a good smoke from a Cuban city of the same name, the Havana originated in Great Britain, far from its Caribbean namesake. A man-made breed, the Havana is the result of a 1950s selective breeding programme to maintain the graceful lines of the Siamese without its point pattern.

The original breeders named their creation after the famous cigar, the colour of which it approximates. But suspicions that the breed was not of British origin led to a new name just a few years later: the Chestnut Brown. However, more recently the original name has begun to be commonly used again.

Like its Siamese forebears, the Havana is a smart and loving cat. It is extremely playful and demanding

Below: The Havana has a smooth, glossy coat of rich chestnut brown, and luminous green eyes. The whiskers and nose are the same colour as the coat.

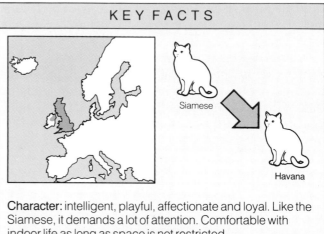

KEY FACTS

Siamese

Havana

Character: intelligent, playful, affectionate and loyal. Like the Siamese, it demands a lot of attention. Comfortable with indoor life as long as space is not restricted.
Care: daily grooming with a gloved hand, in the hair's natural growth direction. No special dietary requirements.
Pedigree faults: marked coat, round head, deformed tail.

of attention and praise. Despite this active nature, it is quite comfortable wih an indoor existence. It generally forms a tight bond with one member of the family and is constantly loyal thereafter.

This is a one-colour breed, but show standards differ between the United States and Great Britain. British enthusiasts prefer a look closer to that of the Orientals, while the Americans prefer something closer to the Russian Blue.

The fur is short, extremely glossy, and even over the entire body. The body is long and thin, with long, thin

legs, small, egg-shaped paws, and a long, tapering tail. The head is wedge shaped (longer than it is wide), with a short, angled nose; it has far-set, almond-shaped, slanted eyes and extremely large ears that are rounded at the tips and pink inside.

Common standard faults are spots or white hairs.

The coat should be brushed and rubbed with a gloved hand daily, always in the hair's natural growth direction. The Havana is an extremely healthy cat and requires no special diet.

Females make first-rate mothers for their litters of plush-covered kittens. They speak constantly with their new charges. The Havana is a popular breed but remains comparatively rare. As a result, it generally carries a hefty price.

Above: *Elegant and aristocratic in bearing, the Havana has a long, lithe body and whip-like tail. The hind legs are slightly longer than the forelegs.*

BURMESE

THE BURMESE WAS first described as early as 1350 in a book of poems from Thailand (then Siam). It was not until the 1920s, however, that the first specimen made its way out into the world.

A single queen, named Wong Mau, was imported into the United States and crossed with a Siamese tom to begin the cat's new line. Nearly all of today's Burmese are descendants of Wong Mau.

The Burmese has the same affection for people as the Siamese, but is much less vocal. It enjoys people, both those it is familiar with and strangers. It is an intelligent, inquisitive cat that needs praise and attention, as well as regular, daily play time. Highly adaptable to new situations, the Burmese enjoys travel, especially when allowed to watch the countryside roll by. It is a good mouser and one of our longer-lived breeds, reaching ages up to 18 years.

There are four varieties recognized on both sides of the Atlantic, all with gold to yellow eyes: Brown (Sable in America), warm seal brown shading to lighter;

Below: *One of the more recent colours, the Lilac is a pale dove grey with a slight pinkish hint.*

The kittens are almost white when first born.

132

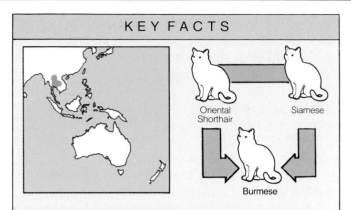

Oriental
Shorthair

Siamese

Burmese

Character: enjoys human contact, makes an affectionate companion. Adaptable to both indoor and outdoor life, likes plenty of play and exercise. Long life expectancy.
Care: daily grooming with a gloved hand to maintain glossy coat. Supplement diet with vitamins. Exercise and play are important in daily routine.

Chocolate (Brown in America); Blue, blue-grey with fawn shading and lighter underside; Lilac, pink-grey. In Britain the whole range of Tortoiseshell variations is also recognized.

The fur is short and satiny. The body is medium in length and muscular in build, with forelegs longer than hindlegs; it has small, egg-shaped paws and a medium-length tail that ends in a point. The head is round with high cheekbones, a short nose, round eyes, and medium ears that are rounded at the tips.

The glossy coat can be easily maintained with daily stroking with a gloved hand, possibly dampened with water. The Burmese is not a finicky eater. Vitamin supplements are recommended during the growing period. Females generally do not experience problem births, and litters usually include five kittens. The young ones begin life with light brown coats that darken as they age.

Varieties: from left to right, Chocolate, Champagne, Blue, Platinum and Lilac.

Right: The Red Burmese originated from cross-breeding between a Shorthaired ginger tabby, Red-Point Siamese and Tortie-and-White farm cat. The colouring is lighter and less "hot" than in other reds.

JAPANESE BOBTAIL

AN ANCIENT BREED in its native Japan, the Japanese Bobtail is a unique breed. Its name, bobtail, arises because the cat's appendage is only four or five inches in length. It is also curled, with hair growing out of it in all directions, producing a fluffy, bobbed look.

The Japanese Bobtail has the peculiar habit of raising one of its front paws when seated, and Japanese folklore holds that this is a sign of good fortune. Likewise, the Mi-Ke variety (black, red and white, or calico) is a symbol of particularly good luck.

Although references to the cat date back over the centuries, it was not until after World War II that the cat was introduced to the rest of the world. Returning soldiers in the U.S. Armed Services brought several back home with them.

The Japanese Bobtail is an affectionate cat that attaches itself to the entire family. It's also intelligent and inquisitive and demands attention and respect. Play should be part of its routine.

The most popular variety is the Mi-Ke, although the Japanese Bobtail is also popular as Black, White, Red, Black-and-White, Red-and-White, and Tortoiseshell (black, red and cream). It is recognized in any pedigree colour, except the Siamese and Abyssinian patterns.

The fur is soft and silky. The body is slender like the traditional Oriental build but with more muscling. The legs are long, with the hindlegs slightly longer, and end in medium, egg-shaped paws. The head is definitely triangular, with high cheekbones, a long nose, well-developed muzzle and large, oval eyes. The ears are medium sized and rounded at the tips.

Common standard faults are a round head, heavy muscling, too long a tail, or a tail that is not curved.

Light daily brushing is recommended. Fish is the Japanese Bobtail's preferred diet item – understandable in an island breed – and should be given to the cat at least once each week.

This is another comparatively rare breed and can cost a great deal.

Right: With its oval eyes, set at a slant, and high cheekbones, the Bobtail has a distinctive Japanese appearance. Varieties include White, Black, Red, Bicolour (shown here) and Tortoiseshell, but the favoured variety (shown opposite page) is the "Mi-ke" (Japanese for "three-furs"); this has patches of black, red and white, and is a symbol of good luck in its native Japan. The Bobtail is sociable and highly vocal, and will often "converse" with its owner.

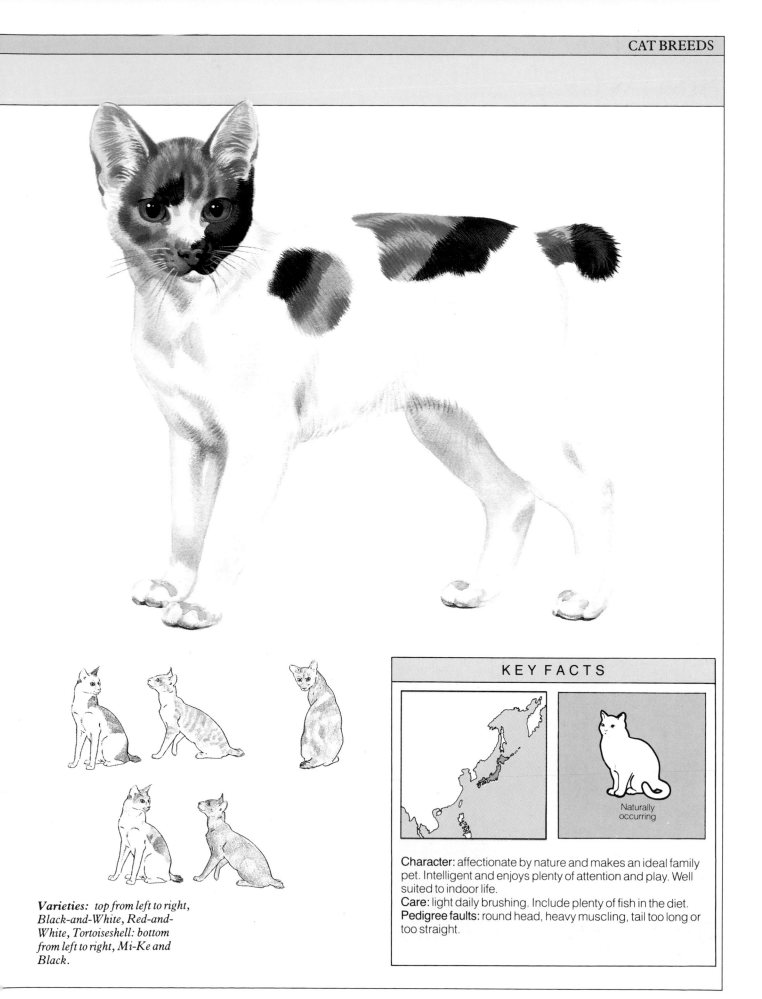

Varieties: top from left to right, Black-and-White, Red-and-White, Tortoiseshell: bottom from left to right, Mi-Ke and Black.

KEY FACTS

Naturally occurring

Character: affectionate by nature and makes an ideal family pet. Intelligent and enjoys plenty of attention and play. Well suited to indoor life.
Care: light daily brushing. Include plenty of fish in the diet.
Pedigree faults: round head, heavy muscling, tail too long or too straight.

SINGAPURA

IN ITS NATIVE Singapore, this breed is referred to as the "Drain Cat," a name that reflects both its lifestyle and the low esteem in which cats are held by the residents there. In short, they just don't have a fondness for cats.

As a result, their land's native street cats have led deprived lives for generations, roaming the streets wild and often seeking shelter in drains. This lifestyle is a probable cause of their smaller bodies, in comparison to those of other Oriental breeds.

Another result of its lifestyle is a reserved tempera-ment that reflects the cat's limited contact with human affection. With patience and gentle handling, the Singapura will come to love human company and lavish its own affection in return, although always in a subdued, quiet manner. Its street ancestry also has equipped the animal to adapt quickly and easily to whatever situation it finds itself in, but it prefers a peaceful, indoor existence.

For the most part, the breed was unappreciated and neglected until American breeders took an interest in it and imported several individuals into the United States. While there are many naturally occurring varieties in Singapore, only ivory ticked with brown, and a white-and-ticked tabby bicolour have surfaced in the United States.

KEY FACTS

Naturally occurring

Character: placid, undemanding and good-natured. Reserved temperament can be overcome with patience and gentle handling. Adaptable, enjoys indoor life.
Care: groom by stroking with a gloved hand. No special dietary requirements.

Varieties: from left to right, Ivory ticked with Brown and Tabby Bicolour.

The fur is short and silky. The body is small and muscular, with a constant slight arch to the back. The legs are medium in length, with small, egg-shaped paws. The tail is medium in length and straight. The head is round with a short nose, extremely large, almond-shaped, slanted eyes, and a fully developed chin. The ears are large and rounded at the tips. The face appears constantly alert.

The coat should be rubbed regularly with a gloved hand, possibly dampened with water. The Singapura eats a wide-ranging diet, which is further evidence that its ancestors were street cats.

Left and above: The Singapura is a small, muscular cat with short, silky, close-lying fur. Although a street cat in its native country, it is very quiet and sweet-natured, not at all "street-wise", and prefers a quiet life indoors.

BOMBAY

THE BOMBAY IS another modern, man-made breed that originated in the 1970s in the United States. It is the result of crossbreeding Burmese and American Shorthairs. The name refers to the Indian city of Bombay because the dense black coat of the breed reminded the breeders of the panther of that Asian country.

Craving companionship as much as any cat breed, the Bombay should not be left alone for extended periods of time. It is extremely affectionate and needs that affection returned regularly. It rarely stops purring. It loves the entire family but also needs time to itself. It is a sedate, peaceful cat that detests loud noises. Created for life in an apartment, it never needs to spend time outdoors.

This is a single colour breed.

The fur is short and close lying, with a sheen that has

Left: *Strikingly handsome, the Bombay looks like a miniature Indian black panther. The lustrous coat is jet black and the huge, saucer eyes are a brilliant copper shade.*

the look of patent leather. The body, legs and tail are all medium in length. The paws are small and egg shaped. The head seems large for the body; it is rounded, with a short nose, a strong chin, round, dazzling, copper eyes, and large ears that are rounded at the tips. It perks its ears at the slightest sounds.

Common standard faults are curly or spotted hair, an abnormal tail, green eyes, and a nose that is not black.

Very gentle, occasional rubbing with a gloved hand is recommended. By comparison to nearly all other breeds, the Bombay has a very small appetite, probably because it burns so few calories in its sedate lifestyle. Kittens do not share this low regard for food and are voracious eaters. They start life with much lighter coats that darken after they are about six months old.

Below: The Bombay has been described as a "patent-leather kid with new-penny eyes"

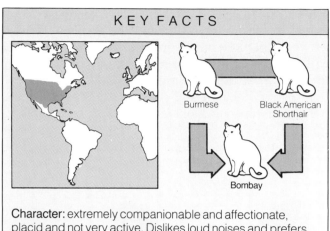

KEY FACTS

Burmese — Black American Shorthair

Bombay

Character: extremely companionable and affectionate, placid and not very active. Dislikes loud noises and prefers life indoors.
Care: occasional stroking with a gloved hand will maintain a glossy coat. Easy to feed.
Pedigree faults: curly or marked coat, abnormal tail, green eyes, a nose that is not black.

TONKINESE

ONE OF OUR newest breeds, the Tonkinese originated in the 1970s in Canada, the result of a cross between Siamese and Burmese parents. It is a cat with point markings similar to the Siamese, but in the Tonkinese these are much less defined.

It is also one of the most affectionate of cats. Sometimes this affectionate quality can be a liability. Early in its life the Tonkinese associates cars with people, and it has a tendency to stray dangerously close to cars. The cat needs to have its affection returned,

Above: *A handsome Blue Mink Tonkinese poses for the camera. These cats are highly inquisitive, outgoing and affectionate and make ideal household pets.*

Varieties: from left to right, Natural Mink, Blue Mink, Honey Mink, Champagne Mink and Platinum Mink.

both in play and in gentle times together with its owner. It also enjoys exercise outside. The Tonkinese travels very well and enjoys watching the passing landscape.

There are five varieties: Natural Mink, brown coat with dark brown markings; Blue Mink, blue-grey coat with slate-blue markings; Honey Mink, deep brown coat with chocolate markings; Champagne Mink, yellow-brown coat with light brown markings; and Platinum Mink, grey coat with darker markings. All have blue-green eyes.

The fur is short, soft and shiny. The body is medium sized and slender, with comparatively long legs ending in small, egg-shaped paws. The head is rounded with a long nose, a square muzzle, almond-shaped, slightly slanted eyes, and large ears that are rounded at the tips.

Regular rubbing with a gloved hand, possibly dampened with water, is recommended to keep the coat clean and shiny. Diet is nonrestrictive.

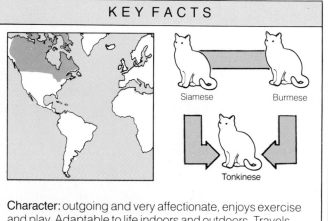

KEY FACTS

Siamese Burmese

Tonkinese

Character: outgoing and very affectionate, enjoys exercise and play. Adaptable to life indoors and outdoors. Travels well and has a long life expectancy.
Care: rubbing with a gloved hand keeps the coat shiny. No special dietary requirements.

Right: The Tonkinese was the first pedigree breed to originate in Canada. It is the result of a cross between a Siamese and a Burmese, and combines the dark points of the former with the dark coat of the latter. As with the Burmese, the kittens are born with a very light coat, which gradually darkens. This one is a Champagne Mink.

SNOWSHOE

A VERY RECENTLY developed breed, the Snowshoe is a man-made creation resulting from a cross between the Siamese and the Bicolour American Shorthair. No show standards have yet been established, although when they are set they will certainly include the snow white paws to which it owes its name.

This Siamese-like cat is generally an active animal that has a great deal of affection for the whole family. It seems most at ease with an indoor existence.

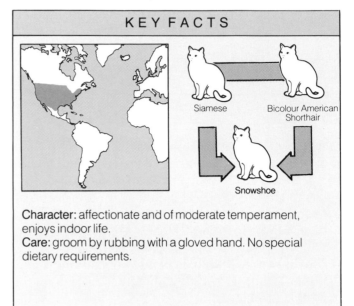

KEY FACTS

Siamese → Bicolour American Shorthair → Snowshoe

Character: affectionate and of moderate temperament, enjoys indoor life.
Care: groom by rubbing with a gloved hand. No special dietary requirements.

Varieties: from left to right, Seal-Point and Blue-Point.

Above and right: *The Snowshoe, so called because of the white mittens on each of its paws, is extremely rare. It looks like a short-haired Birman with its dark points (mask, ears, legs and tail).*

Two varieties have emerged thus far: Seal-Point, with fawn coat with a paler chest and underside, seal-brown points, and snow white paws; and Blue-Point, with blue-white coat with a paler chest and underside, grey-blue points, and snow white paws. The eyes are deep blue.

The fur is short, soft and glossy. The body is slender but muscular with medium length. It has thin legs, round, medium-sized paws, and a medium, tapered tail. The head is triangular with a medium nose and pronounced muzzle, large, almond-shaped eyes, and large, rounded ears.

The coat should be rubbed regularly with a gloved hand. The Snowshoe has no special diet requirements.

REX

KEY FACTS

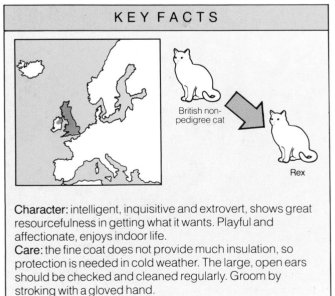

British non-pedigree cat

Rex

Character: intelligent, inquisitive and extrovert, shows great resourcefulness in getting what it wants. Playful and affectionate, enjoys indoor life.
Care: the fine coat does not provide much insulation, so protection is needed in cold weather. The large, open ears should be checked and cleaned regularly. Groom by stroking with a gloved hand.

THERE ARE ACTUALLY two breeds of this curly-coated cat: the Cornish Rex and the Devon Rex. The name Rex was borrowed from that given to a similar curly mutation in rabbits.

The first Cornish Rex appeared in 1950 in a litter of farm kittens in Cornwall in Great Britain. Among the normal kittens was one red-and-white male with a wavy coat and curly whiskers. A local vet suggested that the mutation be bred back to its mother, and the result was a litter of several curly-coated cats.

Another curly-coated cat appeared in an otherwise normal litter in 1960, this time in the neighbouring county of Devon. Initial assumptions were that this mutation was related to the earlier one in Cornwall, but interbreeding efforts failed to produce curly-coated kittens. Thus, it was revealed that the Devon Rex and Cornish Rex mutations are the results of different genes. Rex cats were officially recognized in Britain in the 1960s and in the 1970s in the States.

Varieties: from left to right, Brown, Red, Black, Blue and Tortoiseshell.

Both the Cornish Rex and the Devon Rex are affectionate, energetic cats that enjoy gentle play and can even be mischievous in creating their own games. The Devon Rex has the curious habit of wagging its tail like a dog when it's happy. This attribute, combined with the curly coat, has earned it the nickname of the "Poodle Cat." The ideal owner for either Rex shares their gentle natures.

All colours and patterns are recognized in both Rexes, with the exception of Bicolour in the Devon (although Tortoiseshell and White is permitted); in the Cornish asymmetrical white markings are allowed. The eye colour should complement that of the coat. Those with Siamese point patterns are referred to as the Si-Rex.

The fur of the Cornish Rex is curly, fine, and silky. The body is long and quite slender with a constant slight-to-advanced arch in the back and curl in the long, thin tail. The legs are very long and thin, with small, egg-shaped paws. The head is wedge shaped with a well-developed nose and muzzle, medium, egg-shaped eyes, and large ears that are pointed.

*Despite their similarities in origin and appearance, the Cornish and Devon Rex cats are two distinct breeds. The Devon Rex **left** has a curlier but thinner coat than its Cornish counterpart **above**. The Devon also has a unique wide-cheeked pixie-like head and huge bat-wing ears.*

Devon Rex fur is slightly curlier, coarser, and thinner than that of the Cornish Rex. The body is long and slender with a similar arch in the back and curl in the tail. The legs are long and thin, with small, egg-shaped paws. The head is triangular, but wider than that of the Cornish Rex. Nose, muzzle, eyes and ears are similar.

Regular stroking with a gloved hand is advised to maintain the coat. Meat is the favoured food, and the Rex will take every opportunity to overeat, which quickly results in unwanted weight gain on its slender frame.

Females make excellent parents, usually having litters of four or five. Kittens seem to be born on the move. They are active and inquisitive from a very early age.

EGYPTIAN MAU

CATS THAT LOOK exactly like today's Egyptian Mau are depicted in art that dates from 1400 B.C. in Egypt. A first-cousin of the Abyssinian, the Egyptian Mau is also reputed to be the direct descendant of the sacred Temple cats, but it is also possible – even likely – that the modern cat was bred to resemble the sacred Temple cats. The name, "Mau," is borrowed from the ancient Egyptian civilization, where it meant cat.

The Egyptian Mau is a naturally occurring breed in Egypt. The first to leave their native land were taken to Italy from Cairo in the early 1950s by Princess Natalie Troubetskoye. She then took offspring of the cats with her to the United States in 1956.

It is an affectionate and playful cat, although delicate of constitution. It does not adapt well to cold temperatures or to the change of seasons. However, it is an able mouser. The Egyptian Mau also makes its own decisions about who it likes and who it doesn't like. It adapts to almost any living condition and needs no

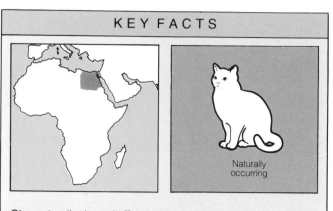

KEY FACTS

Naturally occurring

Character: lively and affectionate, though somewhat aloof with strangers. Has a melodious voice. An able mouser, but is well suited to life indoors.
Care: requires protection from cold temperatures. Feed on meat and giblets. Gentle stroking with a gloved hand will maintain the coat.

Left and far right: Similar in build to the Abyssinian, the Egyptian Mau has a powerful, muscular body and sleek, glossy coat. The pattern is subtle and attractive, consisting of random spots that sometimes run together to form broken stripes, and the tail and legs are banded. The two shown here are of the Bronze variety, and display the characteristic "M" and frown marks on the forehead and "mascara" lines on the cheeks. The jade green eyes are almond-shaped.

Varieties: from left to right, Smoke, Silver, Bronze and Pewter.

time outdoors.

In all four varieties the markings are random spots about the body. The varieties are: Smoke, with grey coat with white undercoat and black markings; Silver, with silver-grey coat with dark grey markings; Bronze, with light brown coat with dark brown markings; and Pewter, with light fawn coat with brown or grey markings. All should have a scarab beetle pattern on their brows.

The fur is dense but finely textured. The body is medium length and muscular, with medium legs and small, egg-shaped paws. The head is triangular, with a short nose, large, almond-shaped eyes and large, slightly pointed ears.

Common standard faults are no spots, a pointed nose, a short tail and nonyellow or nonhazel eyes.

The Egyptian Mau prefers a diet of meat with occasional giblets. Gentle stroking with a gloved hand is advised to maintain the coat. The breed needs special help to get through the change in seasons and periods of cold temperature.

Both sexes are good parents, taking the best of care of their kittens and spending great amounts of time playing with them.

SPHYNX

THE SPHYNX IS, beyond any argument, the most unusual breed of cat. Unlike every other breed, it is hairless. It is quite rare, and only a few groups officially recognize it for show.

The first Sphynx appeared as a hairless kitten in a litter of otherwise normal, short-haired kittens in Canada in 1966. Although it is the breed that continues today, this was not the first time that a hairless mutation has occurred. A breed, dubbed the Mexican Hairless, was bred for a short time in Mexico in the late 19th century.

Affectionate and sociable, the Sphynx adapts well to any owner that will respect its desire for peace and quiet. It prefers not to be held tightly or cuddled. It should be kept indoors at all times and is best suited to a temperate climate, as it is susceptible to temperature-related illnesses.

Those organizations that recognize the Sphynx accept it in any colour and pattern, with eye colour that complements that of the coat.

The breed is hairless with very fine, black, downlike fur on the face, ears, paws, tail, and back. The body is long and slender, made to appear even more so by the lack of hair, with a long, tapered tail. The legs are long and slender, with small, round paws. The head is an elongated triangle, with a short nose, pouty chin, large, almond-shaped eyes, and very large, very pointed ears.

Common standard faults are extremely wrinkled skin and downlike hair on the body.

KEY FACTS

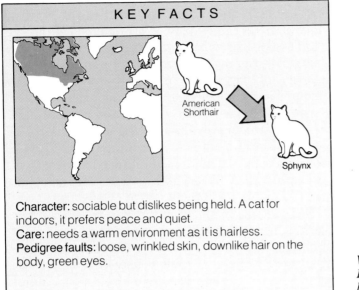

American Shorthair → Sphynx

Character: sociable but dislikes being held. A cat for indoors, it prefers peace and quiet.
Care: needs a warm environment as it is hairless.
Pedigree faults: loose, wrinkled skin, downlike hair on the body, green eyes.

Varieties: top from left to right, Black, Siamese and Red: bottom from left to right, Tabby, Blue-and-Cream and Blue Bicolour.

Left and right: The Sphynx is sometimes known as the hairless Cat, but does in fact have a thin covering of down-like hair that feels like suede. Something of an acquired taste, perhaps, but the cat is gentle and affectionate, with a sweet expression. This is a controversial breed, recognized only by a few of the smaller North American cat associations.

EUROPEAN SHORTHAIR

KEY FACTS

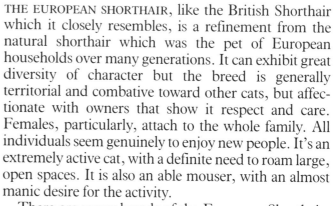

Best of European non-pedigree cats

European Shorthair

Character: friendly and outgoing, makes a good family pet. Territorial and intolerant of other cats. An able mouser, extremely active, enjoys roaming large, open spaces. Long life expectancy.

Care: regular brushing with a gloved hand will keep the coat sleek and glossy. Enjoys meat and milk.

THE EUROPEAN SHORTHAIR, like the British Shorthair which it closely resembles, is a refinement from the natural shorthair which was the pet of European households over many generations. It can exhibit great diversity of character but the breed is generally territorial and combative toward other cats, but affectionate with owners that show it respect and care. Females, particularly, attach to the whole family. All individuals seem genuinely to enjoy new people. It's an extremely active cat, with a definite need to roam large, open spaces. It is also an able mouser, with an almost manic desire for the activity.

There are many breeds of the European Shorthair: Black, which is extremely widespread and has a glossy black coat with yellow, orange or copper eyes; White, with snow white coat with yellow or copper eyes; Albino, with white coat with light blue eyes and pupils that reflect red; Cream, which is extremely rare and has a uniform cream coat with copper or hazel eyes.

Varieties: from left to right, White, Red, Tortoiseshell, Brown Tabby and Tortoiseshell-and-White.

Left: *The European White is a magnificent animal, and relatively rare. All European Shorthairs are hardy and resistant to cold, thanks to their dense, warm coat.*

Above: *The European Tabby has a stocky, muscular body, pronounced cheeks and broad shoulders. It is also an inveterate mouser.*

Red, with red-brown coat with orange eyes; Grey, with grey coat with orange or copper eyes; Tabby, tiger-striped; Marbled, see Classic Tabby pattern under American Shorthair; Tortie, with black, red and cream coat with copper, orange or hazel eyes; Tortie-with-White, with black, red and cream coat with white on face and chest, and orange, amber, or copper eyes; Blue-Cream, with blue and cream coat with orange, yellow or copper eyes; Black-and-White Bicolour; White-and-Blue Bicolour; Orange-and-White Bicolour; and Cream-and-White Bicolour.

The fur is short, thick, fine textured, and sometimes bristly. The body is extremely muscular and sturdy, with similar legs and medium, round paws. The head is round with a short nose, fully developed cheeks, large, round eyes, and relatively small, pointed ears.

Regular brushing and stroking with a gloved hand will maintain the coat. The European Shorthair will eat anything but prefers meat and milk. It is a very long-lived cat.

These breeds, if given the slightest opportunity, will reproduce more frequently than any other breeds. They will also produce much larger litters.

SCOTTISH FOLD

IN 1961 ON a farm in Scotland, several cats with folded ears were born. Hence, the name of this unique breed. The folded-ear trait may have actually been brought to Great Britain about a century earlier by a sailor returning from China. The Chinese cat with the first nonerect ears received much public attention, but records are not firm about whether it produced a line of direct descendants. So the 1961 births are considered the beginnings of today's Scottish Fold.

While the breed origins are firmly British, organizations in the U.K. do not officially recognize the cat because of potential hearing problems that can be caused by the forward-folded ears. The breed is fully recognized in the United States.

It is an extremely affectionate cat that enjoys nothing more than the home life. However, attesting to its farm beginnings, it is an able mouser and appreciates the occasional outing. It makes a special friend of one member of the family, but also shows its affection for other people.

Varieties include most of those already described for the American Shorthair: Black, Blue, Red, Cream, White, Smoke, Shaded, Chinchilla, Tortie, Classic Tabby, Mackerel Tabby and Bicolour.

The fur is short, dense and soft. The body is short and rounded, with short, muscular legs and medium, round paws and a short, thick tail. The head is large and round, with large, round eyes and a pronounced nose. The ears – this breed's distinguishing characteristics – are small and folded forward.

Common standard faults are kinked tail, erect ears, and small head.

Regular brushing will maintain the coat. No special diet is necessary. Kittens do not reveal whether they have inherited the folded ears until after their first month of life.

KEY FACTS

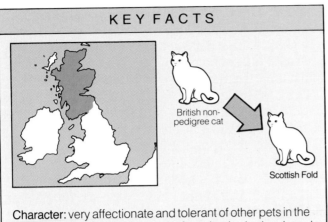

British non-pedigree cat

Scottish Fold

Character: very affectionate and tolerant of other pets in the household. Enjoys the home comforts, but is also hardy and an able mouser.
Care: easy to feed and care for. Brush regularly to maintain the coat. Check and clean the ears regularly.
Pedigree faults: kinked tail, erect ears, small head.

Below: The wide-eyed and slightly sad expression of the Scottish Fold belies its robust and playful nature. It is an affectionate and resilient cat and an excellent mouser.

Varieties: from left to right, Cream with orange eyes, Black Smoke, Silver Tabby, Blue-Cream and Red Bicolour.

Right: The Scottish Fold is the result of an extremely rare genetic mutation. The breed is officially banned in Britain, but popular in the United States, where it is bred in an unlimited range of colours.

MALAYAN

THE MALAYAN IS a very recent breed. It originated in the United States, where it was officially recognized in 1980. It differs from the Burmese only in colour and is classed as Burmese in Great Britain. Malayan kittens are regularly and naturally produced as part of Burmese litters.

Above: *The Blue Tortie is a mixture of blue and cream. It has not yet achieved recognition.*

It is an extremely affectionate cat towards owners, family and friends and even towards strangers. However, it needs to have that affection returned, and it needs quite a bit of play time included in its routine. Hating loud noises, the Malayan nevertheless enjoys travel.

There are three varieties: Blue, blue-grey with fawn hint; Platinum, silver-grey with fawn hint; and Champagne, yellow-brown. All have yellow eyes.

The fur is short, fine, and soft. The body is stocky and muscular with medium-length, muscular legs and large, round paws. The tail is medium length. The head is round with a short nose, wide-set, round eyes, and large, rounded ears.

Common standard faults are nonyellow eyes, white markings and a kinky tail.

Regular stroking with a gloved hand will maintain the glossy sheen of the coat: Meat is a preferred food. Vitamin supplements are recommended for growing animals.

Left: *The Malayan is strictly an American breed and differs from the Burmese only in colour. The body is hard and muscular with a strong, rounded chest and the head has a pleasing shape with round, wide-set eyes. Shown here is the Champagne variety.*

Varieties: *from left to right, Blue, Platinum and Champagne.*

KEY FACTS

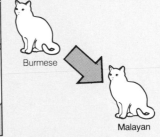

Burmese

Malayan

Character: very friendly and outgoing, likes a lot of attention. Adaptable to indoor and outdoor life; and likes to travel. Dislikes loud noises.

Care: no special dietary requirements, but vitamin supplements are recommended for growing animals. Groom by stroking with a gloved hand. Needs plenty of play and exercise in its daily routine.

OCICAT

THE OCICAT TAKES its name from the wild Ocelot, whose spotted coat it resembles. To achieve this look the Ocicat was bred from pedigree Abyssinians, Siamese and American Shorthairs.

It is an active cat that needs outdoor periods and plenty of play when indoors. It is also affectionate and among the few breeds that will walk on a leash like a dog.

The coat is cream-grey with irregular brown markings throughout. The fur is short and thick. The body is large and muscular, with muscular legs and large, egg-shaped paws. The tail is long and tapered. The head is round with a pronounced muzzle, large, round eyes, and very large, pointed ears.

A common standard fault is a coat that resembles the Classic Tabby Pattern too closely.

Regular brushing is all that's needed to maintain the shiny coat. Meat and fish, offered alternately, provide the basis of the diet.

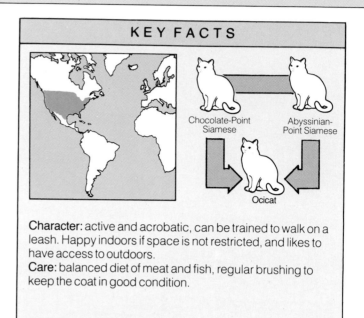

KEY FACTS

Chocolate-Point Siamese   Abyssinian-Point Siamese

Ocicat

Character: active and acrobatic, can be trained to walk on a leash. Happy indoors if space is not restricted, and likes to have access to outdoors.
Care: balanced diet of meat and fish, regular brushing to keep the coat in good condition.

Left: The Ocicat was bred from an Abyssinian-Point Siamese and a Chocolate-Point Siamese, but it also has American Shorthairs in its lineage, so it tends to be larger and heavier than other Oriental breeds. The main colours are cream with chestnut-brown spots and cream with light chocolate spots. Silver and Bronze are more recent varieties.

Above: With its sleek, strikingly spotted coat, long legs and golden yellow eyes, the Ocicat looks like a miniature Ocelot – hence its name.

INDEX

CREDITS

Quarto would like to thank the following for their help with this publication and for permission to reproduce copyright material. While every effort has been made to trace and acknowledge all copyright holders, we would like to apologize should any omissions have been made.

KEY: r. = right, l. = left, a. = above, b. = below

Title page: Sally Anne Thompson/ Animal Photography; p. 6: a. By courtesy of the Natural History Museum of Los Angeles County, b. Marcus Schneck; p. 7: a. Leonard Rue Enterprises, b. Joe McDonald; p. 9: a. R. Willbie/ Animal Photography, b. Sally Anne Thompson/Animal Photography; p. 10: l.a. Gregory K. Scott, l.b. Ron P. Jaffe/Unicorn Stock Photos, r. Pam Powers/ Unicorn Stock Photos; p. 11: Pam Powers/Unicorn Stock Photos; p. 13: a., l.b. and r.b. Marc Henrie, ASC; p. 15: a.l. Diane Calkins, U.S.A., a.r. Sally Anne Thompson/Animal Photography;

p. 17: Joe McDonald; p. 18: a. Rosemary Shelton; pp. 18/19: b. Aneal Vohra/Unicorn Stock Photos; p. 19: a. Rod Furgason/ Unicorn Stock Photos; p. 20: a. Ronald E. Partis/Unicorn Stock Photos, Gerald L. Wicklund; p. 21: Gerald L. Wicklund; p. 22: a. Gerald L. Wicklund, b. Jim Riddle/Unicorn Stock Photos; p. 23: a. Joe McDonald, b. Gregory K. Scott; p. 24: a.l. Jeanetta K. Hodges, b. Fred Preisler; pp. 24/25: a. Joe & Carol McDonald; p. 25: a. Ken Stevens/ Unicorn Stock Photos; p. 26: a.l. Sally Anne Thompson/Animal Photography, a.r. Gerald L. Wicklund; p. 27: a. R. Willbie/ Animal Photography, b. Sally Anne Thompson/Animal Photography; p. 29: Sally Anne Thompson/Animal Photography; p. 30: l. Diane Calkins: r. Gregory K. Scott; p. 31: Joe McDonald; p. 32: Gregory K. Scott; p. 33: l. Diane Calkins, r. Gregory K. Scott; p. 34: J. Bisley/Unicorn Stock Photos; p. 35: a.l. Jay Foreman/Unicorn Stock Photos,

a.r. Gregory K. Scott, b. J. Bisley/ Unicorn Stock Photos; p. 36: l. Rosemary Shelton, r. Gregory K. Scott; p. 37: Sally Anne Thompson; p. 38: H. Schmeiser/ Unicorn Stock Photos; p. 39: C. Strock; p. 40: b. Rosemary Shelton; pp. 40/41: a. Joe McDonald; p. 41: Sally Anne Thompson; p. 43: a. Jay Foreman, b. Ronald E. Partis; p. 44: Pam Powers/Unicorn Stock Photos; p. 45: Ronald E. Partis/Unicorn Stock Photos; p. 46: a. J. Bisley, b. C. Strock; p. 49: C. Strock; p. 50: Aneal Vohra/Unicorn Stock Photos; p. 51: Marc Henrie, ASC; p. 52: Deneve Feigh Bunde/ Unicorn Stock Photos; p. 54: a. Sally Anne Thompson/Animal Photography, b. Marc Henrie, ASC; p. 55: Diane Calkins; p. 56: Joe McDonald; p. 57: Gregory K. Scott; p. 58: Jim Riddle/Unicorn Stock Photos; p. 59: a. Rosemary Shelton, b. Diane Calkins; p. 61: a. J. Bisley/Unicorn Stock Photos, b. Victor E. Horne/Unicorn Stock Photos; pp. 64, 65, 68, 69, 70, 71, 73, 75, 78, 79, 82, 83, 85, 87,

88, 89, 90, 91, 93: Marc Henrie, ASC; p. 95: a: Animals Unlimited, b. Marc Henrie, ASC; p, 96: Marc Henrie, ASC; p. 97: Crezentia Allen; p. 99: Animals Unlimited; pp. 101, 102, 104, 105, 106, 107, 108, 109, 111: Marc Henrie, ASC; p. 113: Robert Pearcy/Animals; pp. 114/115: Crezentia Allen; pp. 116, 117, 119: Marc Henrie, ASC; pp. 120/121: Animals Unlimited; pp. 122, 123, 124, 125, 127, 128, 129, 130, 131, 132, 133: Marc Henrie, ASC; p. 134: Crezentia Allen; p. 137: a. Animals Unlimited, b. Robert Pearcy/ Animals Animals; p. 138: Marc Henrie, ASC; pp. 139, 140/141: Animals Unlimited; p. 145: Marc Henrie, ASC; p. 146: Animals Unlimited; p. 147: Marc Henrie, ASC; pp. 148/149: Animals Unlimited; p. 150: l. Margo Conte/ Animals Animals, r. Joe McDonald; p. 153: Marc Henrie, ASC; pp. 154/155: Animals Unlimited; p. 156: Marc Henrie, ASC; p. 157: Robert Pearcy/ Animals Animals.